SLOW COOKING

In Crock-Pot,® Slow Cooker, Oven and Multi-Cooker

Revised Edition

Joanna White

BRISTOL PUBLISHING ENTERPRISES
San Leandro, California

A nitty gritty® Cookbook

Printed in the United States of America.

ISBN: 1-55867-252-4

Cover design: Frank J. Paredes
Cover photography: John A. Benson
Food stylist: Susan De Vaty
Illustrations: James Balkovek

CONTENTS

SLOW COOKING TIPS

Slow cookers are ideal for today's busy lifestyles. Prepare the recipe the night before or in the morning, put the cooker on before you leave and have your meal ready to eat when you get home after a long day. Count the advantages and you'll go back to that slow cooker in your cupboard, or invest in a new one.

When I first began this project, I reviewed the handful of books currently available on the subject of slow cooking (sometimes called Crock-Pot® cooking). Many of those books have recipes similar to each other. My goal was to present the reader with a new collection of delicious slow cooking recipes that not only provide variety, but are in tune with today's thinking about food. I hope you enjoy them.

THE ADVANTAGES OF SLOW COOKING

A slow cooker allows the cook to prepare the meal in advance, and to use less time for cleanup. Moreover, when using the low setting, you can leave without worry about having to tend the food. Low heat will not dry out or burn it. Generally, you do not even have to stir. Exact timing is not crucial, so if you are delayed, your food will not be overdone.

More nutrients are retained because of the lower temperatures used. Food is generally more juicy because slow cooking seals in moisture.

Considerably less energy is used (less than a 100-watt bulb) when cooking on the low setting. Slow cookers are ideal in the summer because they do not heat the kitchen.

Slow cookers need little space, making them ideal for R.V.'s and small kitchens.

Slow cookers are good for buffets and informal entertaining because they allow you to serve directly from the pot. Use as you would a chafing dish to keep food warm or to serve hot drinks.

DO'S AND DON'T'S OF SLOW COOKING

- Do not take the lid off during the cooking process unless the recipe calls for it. This will let out steam which is used to cook the food at the top of the pot and it will take at least 15 minutes to regain that steam pressure. Also, positively never remove the lid during the first 2 hours of baking in the slow cooker.
- Always allow more time when cooking at higher altitudes.
- Always bake on the high temperature setting.
- Low temperature refers to 200° F. High temperature refers to 300° F. If your particular brand of slow cooker has additional settings, determine these temperature settings so you can properly follow the recipes in this book.
- Defrost food before using in recipes. Frozen food may cause the slow cooker to crack if using a porcelain, enamel or crockery-lined pot. Also, frozen food

will increase cooking time considerably.

- Be cautious when baking, where another pan is placed in the pot and water is added. Check the pot to make sure the water does not evaporate.
- Do not immerse any electrical control units or parts in water at any time.
- For easier cleanup, spray the pot with nonstick vegetable spray before cooking.
- To maintain the finish on the inside of the pot, soak with warm, soapy water and then scrub with a nylon or plastic pad.
- Root vegetables like carrots, turnips, parsnips, rutabagas, etc., quite often take longer to cook than the meat, so it is best to layer these on the bottom and let the liquid keep the vegetables moist (which helps them cook more evenly).
- Beans are ideal for slow cookers. I like to soak the beans overnight; discard the soaking water and then add the beans to the recipe and slow cook until beans are tender.
- Pasta and rice have a tendency to fall apart or become gummy, so add these ingredients precooked (using conventional cooking methods) at the end of the cooking time or simply serve with the dish.
- Dairy products like milk and sour cream should be added toward the last hour of cooking because slow cooking has a tendency to curdle these products.

- For best results, fill your slow cooker at least half full of ingredients.

METHODS FOR CONVERTING RECIPES TO SLOW COOKERS

There may be variations in cooking temperatures depending on the particular brand of slow cooker, so first determine the proper low (200°) and high (300°) temperature settings. NEVER allow the cooking temperature to drop to less than 180°, in order to prevent spoilage or improperly cooked food.

Generally quadruple the regular cooking in a slow cooker on low. For example, for a stew which requires 2 to 2½ hours standard cooking time, you would increase the time to 8 to 10 hours on low heat.

If choosing to cook on high temperature, double the conventional cooking time but do not leave the slow cooker unattended. You may also need to stir occasionally. The equivalent of 1 hour on high heat is 2 hours on low heat.

Some brands have very high settings to be used for the purpose of browning meats. After browning, be sure to reduce the temperature to low. Or, for meats that need browning, such as chicken, slow cook the food first, and then remove and brown in a hot oven or broiler just before serving.

If you are afraid of not being able to return in time or if cooking time is less than your working day, consider investing in an automatic timer. Your slow cooker plugs into the timer which will turn on automatically after you leave. It is best not have it turn off automatically, because hot food should not be left out for more than 2 hours.

When adapting a recipe to slow cooking, you may need to increase spices. Because the food tends to lose less liquid from evaporation, the extra juiciness may require additional flavoring.

Baking usually requires placing the ingredients in a separate container (like a coffee can, a pudding mold, a tall baking dish, etc.), covering with foil, tying down the foil and surrounding with water.

For thickening sauces: Set cooker on high heat; stir in thickener mixed with cold water and cook for 20 to 30 minutes, stirring occasionally until thickened.

Cornstarch: Use 2 tbs. dissolved in 2 tbs. cold water for every 2 cups of sauce that needs to be thickened.

Flour: Use ¼ cup dissolved in ¼ cup cold water for every 2 cups of sauce that needs to be thickened.

Tapioca: This is usually stirred in before cooking, so it doesn't need to be mixed with water. Use 3 to 4 tbs. for every 2 cups of liquid used in the recipe.

Potato: Sometimes sauces can be thickened by simply adding instant potato flakes or adding pureed potatoes.

TECHNIQUES FOR REDUCING FAT AND SALT IN SLOW COOKING

- Quite often fat is needed to brown meats or onions before cooking. Generally in slow cooking this whole step can be eliminated, so disregard the fat entirely.
- If fat is required to soften the vegetables, substitute chicken stock or water to wilt vegetables.
- Trim excess fat off meats before cooking.
- For high-fat meats like hamburger and sausage, fry in a skillet and drain off fat before adding to your slow cooker.
- Skim fat off top, if visible, or chill meat mixture, let fat solidify and skim fat off.
- Substitute ground turkey for ground beef to reduce fat.
- The best way to reduce salt in your recipe is to replace salt with spices or simply increase the quantity of spices already called for in the recipe. Another method to reduce saltiness is to add white pepper (not black). White pepper is more subtle and takes away from the salty flavor.
- Use low-sodium canned foods and when the recipe calls for garlic salt or celery salt, use powdered garlic or celery instead (increasing the quantity somewhat).
- You can reduce the salty flavor in food by adding chunks of peeled potato which will absorb the salt and remove the chunks before serving the dish.

TYPES OF SLOW COOKERS

I used a variety of slow cookers to test recipes for this book. Slow cookers come in many different shapes and sizes. They range from one solid unit, to separate liners with heating shells, to hot plates with pans on top. Technically, an electric skillet can be used as a slow cooker. Many new versions have deep frying attachments that can reach very high temperatures. A pot that separates from the heating unit for ease of cleaning and storage is a desirable feature.

Slow cooking can also be done in the oven using a casserole, a Dutch oven or other ovenproof container with a tight fitting lid. Cook on low setting (200°) by quadrupling the time for conventional stovetop cooking. A stew that requires 2 to 2½ hours would be increased to 8 to 10 hours. Cook on high setting (300°) in the oven by doubling the time. Be aware that using the oven to cook slowly does not save energy, as a slow cooker does, and is therefore less economical.

Follow your manufacturer's instructions when caring for your slow cooker. Here are some of the surfaces that were used for testing:

Crockery lining. Usually made from glazed stoneware or earthenware, this should be washed (or at least soaked) soon after using. If the slow cooker has a separate liner, it usually can be put in a dishwasher (never immerse the outer electrical unit). Use nylon or plastic scrubbers to remove dried food or stains.

Aluminum lining. I do not advise using aluminum for health reasons and also limitations in cooking high-acid foods. If you have one, wash it with soapy water, use nylon pads and always season with oil before using.

Porcelain or baked enamel lining. More care is required. Be careful to cool completely before washing. Never use abrasive cleansers, only use nylon scrubbers and rinse very well before heating to avoid staining.

Glass or Corning Ware. This surface is ideal for slow cooking because it absorbs heat rapidly, withstands extreme temperatures and sudden temperatures, is easy to clean and holds heat a long time. Avoid metal scouring pads.

Stainless steel is good for heat retention and generally easy to clean. Avoid using steel wool to clean because it can scratch the surface.

Nonstick coating. Use nylon or plastic utensils and definitely do not use anything other than nylon or plastic scrubbers. Most nonstick coatings need to be seasoned before using. Follow the manufacturer's directions for maintenance.

APPETIZERS

HONEY CHICKEN WINGS

This is a wonderful appetizer that can be kept warm and served from the slow cooker at a buffet.

3 lb. chicken wings
salt and pepper to taste
1 cup honey
3 tbs. ketchup
1/2 cup soy sauce
2 tbs. vegetable oil
1 clove garlic, minced
sesame seeds for garnish, optional

Disjoint chicken wings and discard tips. Sprinkle wing parts with salt and pepper. Place honey, ketchup, soy sauce, oil and garlic in the slow cooker and stir until mixed well. Add seasoned chicken wings and stir. Set slow cooker on low heat and cook 5 to 6 hours. If desired, garnish with a sprinkling of sesame seeds.

BARBECUED CHICKEN WINGS

This barbecue sauce is absolutely delicious. Use it with other meats, such as strips of steaks, chicken nuggets, pork medallions, etc.

4 lb. chicken wings
2 large onions, chopped
2 cans (6 oz. each) tomato paste
2 large cloves garlic, minced
1/4 cup Worcestershire sauce
1/4 cup any variety vinegar

1/2 cup brown sugar, packed
1/2 cup sweet pickle relish
1/2 cup red or white wine
2 tsp. salt
2 tsp. dry mustard

Cut off wing tips and discard. Cut wings at the joint and place in the slow cooker. Add remaining ingredients and stir. Set slow cooker on low heat and cook for 5 to 6 hours. Serve directly from pot at a buffet with lots of napkins!

VARIATION: BARBECUED CHICKEN DINNER

Substitute 1 whole chicken, 3 1/2 lb., cut into serving pieces, for chicken wings. Makes 4-6 servings.

TERIYAKI CHICKEN WINGS

This is a quick recipe for teriyaki that takes just minutes to prepare. You can also substitute whole skinned chicken pieces for a tender chicken teriyaki dinner.

2 lb. chicken wings
1 small onion, chopped
1/2 cup light soy sauce
1/2 cup brown sugar, packed
1 tsp. ground ginger
1-2 cloves garlic, minced
2 tbs. dry sherry

Disjoint chicken wings and discard tips (or use them in stock). Place wing parts in the slow cooker. In a separate bowl, combine onion, soy sauce, sugar, ginger, garlic and sherry. Pour mixture over chicken wings and set slow cooker on low heat. Cook for about 5 to 6 hours. If possible, gently stir halfway through cooking process to insure that all wings are coated with sauce.

HUMMUS DIP

Hummus is a Middle Eastern vegetarian dip that has become very popular. I experimented using canned beans versus slow cooked beans and the results were far better with the slow cooker. For variety, add chopped cilantro.

1/4 lb. dried garbanzo beans
water to cover beans
1 tbs. olive oil
1 small onion, chopped
2 cloves garlic, minced

1/2 tsp. ground turmeric
2 tbs. chopped fresh parsley
salt to taste
1-2 tbs. lemon juice, or more to taste

Rinse dried beans under cold running water. Place in the slow cooker and cover with water, making sure that you have at least 2 inches of water on top of beans. Set cooker on low heat and cook for 8 to 10 hours. Drain beans; discard water and rinse under cold water. Drain well. With a food processor or blender, puree beans until about the consistency of mayonnaise. If mixture appears too coarse, add a little water. In a skillet, heat olive oil and sauté onion and garlic until soft and transparent. Add turmeric and cook for an additional minute. Add this mixture to pureed beans in food processor workbowl and blend. Add parsley, salt and lemon juice to taste.

HOT ARTICHOKE DIP

This incredible dip goes well with thick, mild-flavored crackers or slices of crusty French bread. Slow cookers are ideal for keeping food warm, especially at buffet parties.

2 jars (14³⁄₄ oz. each) marinated artichoke hearts, drained
1 cup mayonnaise, fat-free if desired
1 cup sour cream, low-fat or fat-free if desired
2 cups grated Parmesan cheese
1 cup chopped water chestnuts
¹⁄₄ cup finely chopped green onion, or more to taste

Cut artichoke hearts into small pieces. Mix in mayonnaise, sour cream, Parmesan cheese, water chestnuts and green onion. Place in the slow cooker on low heat for at least 1 hour or until thoroughly heated. Serve directly from slow cooker with crackers or sliced French bread.

CHILI CON QUESO (CHEESE DIP)

The slow cooker is great for cheese dip because it can be used on a buffet table to keep the cheese warm. Serve with corn chips or sliced French bread.

2 tbs. butter
2 tbs. finely chopped onion
1-2 cloves garlic, minced
2 fresh tomatoes, peeled and seeded
4 oz. diced green chiles
2½ cups grated Monterey Jack or cheddar cheese

Set the slow cooker on high heat; add butter, onion and garlic and sauté until onion is soft but not brown. Dice tomatoes and add to slow cooker with chiles and cheese. Cook on low heat for 1 hour or until cheese melts completely. Serve directly from slow cooker.

SPICY BEAN DIP

This is a quick and easy vegetarian dip that can be spiced up with the addition of jalapeños. If you're entertaining vegetarian guests, use vegetarian refried beans, which contain animal lard. Serve with corn chips, sliced French bread or crackers.

2 cans (16 oz. each) refried beans*
1 pkg. (1¹/₄ oz.) taco seasoning mix
¹/₂ cup finely chopped onion
2 cups shredded Monterey Jack or cheddar cheese
several drops Tabasco Sauce
jalapeño peppers to taste, optional

Place refried beans, taco seasoning, onion, cheese and Tabasco in the slow cooker and stir. If you wish to really add heat, carefully remove seeds and chop up jalapeño peppers (be careful not to touch your eyes or face) and stir into bean mixture to your personal taste. If mixture appears too thick, add a little water. Cook on low heat until mixture is hot and cheese is melted, about 1 hour. Serve directly from slow cooker.

NOTE: To reduce fat, use low-fat cheese and increase the seasoning slightly.

HOT BACON AND CHEESE DIP

You can't go wrong with bacon and cheese. This is particularly good served with apple and pear slices or thin slices of French bread.

8 slices bacon, diced
8 oz. cream cheese, cubed
2 cups shredded cheddar cheese
6 tbs. half-and-half
1 tsp. Worcestershire sauce
1/4 tsp. dry mustard
1/4 tsp. onion salt
dash Tabasco Sauce

Fry finely diced bacon in a skillet until crisp; drain on paper towels and set aside. Place cream cheese, cheddar cheese, half-and-half, Worcestershire sauce, mustard, onion salt and Tabasco in the slow cooker. Set on low heat and allow cheese to melt slowly, stirring occasionally for approximately 1 hour. Taste and adjust seasonings. Just before guests arrive, stir in bacon and serve directly from slow cooker. If mixture becomes too thick, add more half-and-half to thin. If using apples and pears to accompany this dish, dip fruit slices in lemon juice to help prevent browning.

QUICK HAMBURGER DIP

If you are in a pinch and need something quick to fix for impromptu guests, whip this up and keep it warm in the pot. Serve with tortilla chips, plain crackers or thin slices of French bread.

1 lb. extra lean hamburger
1/2 cup chopped onion
2 cloves garlic, minced
salt to taste
1 can (8 oz.) tomato sauce
1/4 cup ketchup
3/4 tsp. dried oregano
1 tsp. sugar
8 oz. cream cheese
1/3 cup grated Parmesan cheese

In a skillet, brown hamburger with onion; discard fat. Pour browned meat and onion into the slow cooker. Add garlic, salt, tomato sauce, ketchup, oregano, sugar, cream cheese and Parmesan. Set cooker on low heat and serve when cream cheese has melted into mixture, about 1 hour. Stir; taste and adjust seasonings.

FAST FRANKFURTER APPETIZERS

This is so simple it is almost embarrassing! I sometimes mix different types of sausages (bratwurst, kielbasa, Italian, etc), frankfurters or even hot dogs.

3 lb. frankfurters or cooked sausages
1/4 cup brown sugar
1/4 cup water
1/2 cup whiskey or bourbon
1 cup ketchup

Cut frankfurters or sausages into 1-inch pieces. Place frankfurters or sausages in the slow cooker with brown sugar, water, whiskey and ketchup. Set cooker on low heat for 1 hour; taste and increase ketchup if too strong. Serve directly from pot.

HOT HERBY MUSHROOMS

For a change from baked mushrooms, try something healthy and easy to serve.

6 tbs. butter
1 large onion, chopped
2 tsp. dried basil
2 tsp. dried oregano
1/2 tsp. dried thyme
1/4 cup lemon juice
1/2 cup sherry
1/4 tsp. red pepper flakes
3 lb. mushrooms, washed and left whole

Set the slow cooker on high heat. Melt butter; add onion and sauté until onion is limp. Set cooker on low heat. Add spices, lemon juice, sherry and pepper flakes and steep mixture on low heat for 1 to 2 hours. Add mushrooms about 15 minutes before guests arrive. Use toothpicks or a slotted spoon to serve.

HOT CHEESE FONDUE

Beer gives this cheese mixture an unusual zip. Serve with fresh vegetables and corn chips or tortilla chips for dipping. If you really like it hot, add the chopped jalapeño peppers.

1/4 cup flour
2 tsp. chili powder, or to taste
1 lb. Monterey Jack cheese, shredded
1/2 lb. sharp cheddar cheese, shredded
1 can (12 oz.) beer
1 clove garlic, minced
1 can (4 oz.) chopped green chiles
chopped jalapeño peppers to taste, optional

Mix flour with chili powder and toss with shredded cheeses. Pour beer into the slow cooker and cover with shredded cheese mixture. Place garlic, green chiles and jalapeños, if desired, over cheese, but do not stir in until cheese has begun to melt. Set cooker on low heat; warm mixture slowly and stir occasionally. Serve directly from slow cooker.

HOT BEVERAGES

COFFEE MEDITERRANEAN

This mocha mixture, with a tinge of anise and cinnamon, is served hot with a twist of lemon and orange.

2 qt. hot coffee
$1/4$ cup chocolate syrup
$1/3$-$1/2$ cup sugar
2 sticks (6-inch each) cinnamon
2 tsp. whole cloves
$1/2$ tsp. anise flavoring
zest of 1 orange, cut into strips for garnish
zest of 1 lemon, cut into strips for garnish
whipped cream for garnish

Combine coffee, chocolate syrup, sugar, cinnamon, cloves and anise flavoring in the slow cooker. Set on low heat and cook for 45 minutes to 1 hour. Float orange and lemon zest strips that have been tied into knots on top of mixture. Strain liquid into a cup and top each cup with a large dollop of whipped cream.

COFFEE PUNCH

Servings: 30

This is strange combination of coffee, juice and ginger ale works well together.

6 cups coffee
4 cups apple juice or cider
2 cups apricot brandy

1/2 tsp. ground ginger
32 oz. ginger ale

Combine coffee, apple juice or cider, apricot brandy and ginger in the slow cooker. Cook on low heat until hot; add ginger ale and serve immediately.

MULLED CIDER

Servings: 16

This is a sweet, spicy mixture that is loved by all, especially children.

3/4 cup brown sugar, packed
1 tsp. ground cloves
1 tsp. ground allspice

1 tsp. cinnamon
1/4 tsp. salt
1 gal. apple cider

Mix together brown sugar, cloves, allspice, cinnamon and salt. Place mixture in the slow cooker with apple cider and cook on low heat until sugar dissolves. Taste and if mixture is too spicy, add more apple cider.

HOT BRAZILIAN EGGNOG

Usually eggnog is served cold but the Brazilian version is served hot and flavored with coffee.

4 eggs, separated
3 cups milk
2 cups cream
3 tbs. instant coffee
1/2 cup light corn syrup

1/2 cup brandy or rum, or to taste
1/4 cup water
pinch cinnamon, optional
nutmeg for garnish

With an electric mixer, beat egg yolks lightly; beat in milk, cream, instant coffee and 1/4 cup corn syrup. Place mixture in the slow cooker; set on low heat and cook for 30 minutes. Stir in brandy or rum. In a saucepan, heat remaining corn syrup and water to a boil and simmer for 5 minutes. Beat egg whites until soft peaks form and slowly pour corn syrup mixture in a thin stream into eggs. Continue beating until soft peaks form again. Fold mixture into hot milk mixture. Ladle into punch cups or mugs and sprinkle with nutmeg.

FRUITED TEA PUNCH

Serve this spicy, warm punch with orange or lemon slices studded with whole cloves.

5 cups apricot nectar
2 cups orange juice
2 cups water
2 tbs. sugar, or more to taste
2 tsp. cinnamon
pinch ground cloves
4 tsp. instant tea
1 lemon or orange for garnish
whole cloves for garnish

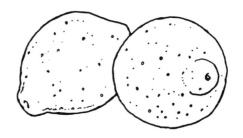

Place apricot nectar, orange juice, water, sugar, cinnamon, and ground cloves in the slow cooker. Heat on low for about 1 hour. Stir in tea. Taste and adjust seasoning or sweetness. Cut lemon into slices and stud rind with whole cloves. Serve by pouring into mugs or glasses and floating a slice of studded fruit on top.

TEA NECTAR

This fruity tea punch is refreshing and soothing.

2 qt. boiling water
8 tea bags, regular or herbal
18 oz. unsweetened pineapple juice
12 oz. apricot nectar
1 can (6 oz.) frozen orange juice
    concentrate, defrosted
6 oz. lemon juice
1 cup sugar
2½ cups water
lemon and lime slices for garnish
maraschino cherries for garnish

Pour boiling water over tea bags and steep for about 5 minutes; remove tea bags and set aside. Pour pineapple juice, apricot nectar, orange juice, lemon juice, sugar and water into the slow cooker. Set on low heat and cook for 1 hour. Stir in tea; taste and adjust sweetness to your personal taste. Float lemon and lime slices and a few maraschino cherries on top for garnish. Serve warm.

CRANBERRY GLOGG

If you are serving children or nondrinkers, you can eliminate the wine from this holiday beverage.

1 qt. cranberry apple juice
2 cups Burgundy wine
³/₄ cup sugar
³/₄ cup water
1 stick (4-inch) cinnamon
3-4 cardamom pods, crushed

6 whole cloves
¹/₂ cup raisins, light and dark mixed
¹/₂ cup whole blanched almonds
zest of 1 orange, cut into strips, for
  garnish

Mix cranberry apple juice, Burgundy, sugar, water, cinnamon stick, cardamom pods and cloves together; cover and chill for 8 to 12 hours. Pour mixture into the slow cooker and cook on low heat for about 1 hour. If desired, you can strain off spices. Add raisins and almonds. Taste and add more cranberry apple juice if too spicy. Float orange zest strips which have been tied into knots on top of mixture for garnish. When serving, be sure to ladle some raisins and almonds into each cup.

NOTE: If you prefer a nonalcoholic drink, substitute 2 cups additional cranberry apple juice and eliminate Burgundy, sugar and water.

MULLED WINE

For wine lovers, this is a must during the holidays.

1 qt. water
12 whole cloves
10 whole allspice
1 stick (6-inch) cinnamon
rinds from 2 oranges
2 tbs. sugar
2 bottles wine, prefer claret
zest of 1 orange, cut into strips for garnish

Place water, cloves, allspice, cinnamon stick, and orange rinds (which have been left in large pieces for easy removal) in the slow cooker. Set cooker on high heat and bring mixture almost to a boil. Add sugar and turn off slow cooker; allow mixture to steep for 45 minutes. Strain off spices and orange rinds; add wine and turn slow cooker on low. Allow mixture to heat to warm and garnish with orange zest strips that have been tied into knots.

HOT PEACH PUNCH

To offer something different during the holidays, try this spicy peach punch.

1 can (46 oz.) peach nectar
20 oz. orange juice
1/2 cup light brown sugar, packed

1 stick (4-inch) cinnamon, in pieces
3/4 tsp. whole cloves
2 tbs. lime juice

Combine nectar, juice and sugar in the slow cooker. Tie cinnamon stick pieces and cloves together in a cheesecloth bag and drop into cooker. Set cooker on low heat and cook for 1 hour before serving. Stir mixture to dissolve sugar. Add lime juice. Taste and adjust sugar or juices if desired. Serve from slow cooker.

GOOD OLD GROG

This grog is a mixture of port and bourbon, sweetened and spiced.

2 qt. ruby port
1 1/2 cups dark raisins
3 sticks (4-inch each) cinnamon

1 1/2 cups bourbon
1/2 cup sugar
12 whole cardamom seeds

Pour port into the slow cooker and stir in raisins and sugar. Tie cardamom seeds and cinnamon sticks in a piece of cheesecloth with a string and set bag in port. Cook on low heat for 2 to 3 hours. Before serving, remove spice bag and add bourbon.

HOT SPIKED APPLE PUNCH

We've all had hot, spiced apple cider, but dress it up with a flavored liqueur or liquor and a dollop of whipped cream and you have pizzazz!

1 gal. apple cider
2 tbs. broken cinnamon sticks
1 tbs. whole cloves
liquor or liqueur of choice: vodka, apple jack,
   apple liqueurs, etc.
allspice for garnish
whipped cream for garnish

Add apple cider, cinnamon sticks and cloves to the slow cooker and cook on low heat for 2 hours. Pour liquor into each cup and add hot spiced apple cider to fill. Sprinkle with allspice and top with a dollop of whipped cream.

HOT SPICED WINE

Serve this directly from the slow cooker, leaving the orange floating for eye appeal. If you wish, add a few slices of lemon for additional garnish.

1 qt. red wine
2/3 cup sugar
1/4 cup lemon juice
1 stick (4-inch) cinnamon
1/4 tsp. nutmeg
1 whole orange
12 whole cloves

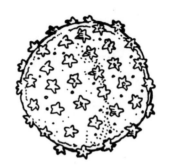

Stir wine, sugar and lemon juice into the slow cooker. Add cinnamon stick and nutmeg. Stud orange with cloves and float in cooker. Set cooker on low heat and simmer for about 1 hour, stirring to make sure sugar has dissolved.

RUSSIAN TEA

If you are always looking for new beverages to serve at parties, this is an unusual warm punch that mixes citrus, almond and spices together.

2 cups water
2 cups sugar
2 cups orange juice
1/4 cup lemon juice
1/2 gal. water
1 tsp. almond extract
2 tsp. vanilla extract
6 whole cloves
2 sticks (3-inch each) cinnamon

In a saucepan, boil water and sugar together for 5 minutes or until sugar dissolves completely. Pour into the slow cooker. Add remaining ingredients. Set cooker on low heat and cook for at least 1 hour before serving. Serve directly from slow cooker.

SOUPS

BLACK BEAN SOUP

Black beans, recently very popular, are healthful and have great flavor. To control "heat," be cautious about the size of the pepper or possibly eliminate it. Use one or more of the suggested garnishes for color. For a higher protein meal, add a ham hock at the start of cooking period and shred meat from bone at end or add cubed cooked ham just before serving.

2 cups dried black beans
6-8 cups chicken, beef or vegetable
   stock
1 large onion, chopped
4 cloves garlic, crushed
1 whole dried red serrano pepper
2 tsp. ground cumin
2 tsp. dried oregano

$1/_2$ tsp. cinnamon
2-3 carrots, sliced
3 stalks celery, sliced
sour cream, chopped tomatoes,
   roasted red pepper sauce, minced
   parsley and/or minced cilantro for
   garnish, optional

Rinse beans and place in the slow cooker. Add broth (use 6 cups for thick soup or 8 cups for thinner soup). Stir in remaining ingredients and cover. Set heat on low and cook for 9 to 10 hours.

HUNGARIAN LAMB SOUP

Lamb soup is a delightful change from the old standard. It is important to use a good paprika, preferably the sweet Hungarian variety.

1/4 cup butter
2 medium onions, chopped
2 lb. lamb shoulder
1 tbs. Hungarian paprika
2 qt. beef stock
2 bay leaves

salt and pepper to taste
2-3 potatoes, peeled and cubed
1/2 cup sliced green beans, fresh or
  frozen
1 tbs. flour
1 cup sour cream

In a skillet, melt butter and add onions. While onions are sautéing, trim lamb of fat and cut into 1-inch cubes. Add lamb to skillet and brown. Stir in paprika and heat for 1 minute. Pour skillet ingredients into the slow cooker with stock, bay leaves, salt and pepper. Set cooker on low heat and cook for 6 to 7 hours. Add potatoes and green beans and cook on low for additional 2 to 3 hours. Half an hour before serving, mix flour with sour cream. Gently stir mixture into soup and heat. Taste and adjust seasonings; remove bay leaves before serving.

TOMATO MINESTRONE

This is a quick and simple version of the traditional Italian soup. You can vary the pastas for a different texture.

2 tbs. olive oil
2 lb. beef shank
1 large onion, chopped
1 cup chopped celery
2 cups tomato sauce
salt and pepper to taste
1 tsp. dried oregano, or more to taste
2 qt. water

1 1/2 cups sliced zucchini
1 cup frozen peas
2 cups cooked orzo pasta, or pasta of
  choice
1 tbs. chopped fresh parsley
grated Parmesan or cheddar cheese for
  garnish

Heat oil in a skillet. Cut shank into large pieces and brown in oil. Place browned meat, onion, celery, tomato sauce, salt, pepper, oregano and water in the slow cooker. Cook on low heat for 6 to 8 hours. Remove meat pieces; discard bones and dice meat into smaller pieces. Return meat to slow cooker; add zucchini and cook for an additional 30 minutes or until zucchini is done. Just before serving, add peas, cooked pasta and parsley. Taste and adjust seasonings. If desired, serve with a sprinkling of Parmesan or cheddar cheese.

SPLIT PEA AND HAM SOUP

This soup is nutritious and filling. The addition of a smoked ham shank gives this recipe a slightly smoky flavor.

4 slices bacon, diced
1 1/2 medium onions, chopped
2 carrots, diced
2 stalks celery, diced
1 lb. dried split peas
1 smoked ham shank

2 bay leaves
3 qt. water
1/4-1/2 tsp. cayenne pepper
salt and pepper to taste
1 cup diced cooked ham
croutons or fresh peas for garnish

In a skillet, cook bacon until crisp; remove and drain on absorbent paper. Sauté onions, carrots, and celery in bacon fat for 5 minutes. Place bacon, sautéed vegetables, peas, ham shank, bay leaves, water, cayenne pepper, salt and pepper in the slow cooker. Set cooker on low heat and cook for 8 to 9 hours or until peas are soft. If you wish to have a smooth texture, puree soup with a food processor or blender and return to slow cooker. Add diced ham before serving and stir until heated through. Taste and adjust seasonings; remove bay leaves. If desired, garnish with croutons or a few fresh peas.

CREAM OF CHESTNUT SOUP

This is a delicious, unique soup, perfect for the holidays, especially as a starter course for an elegant roast goose dinner. If fresh chestnuts are not readily available, use canned chestnuts. Garnish this soup with homemade croutons.

2 lb. fresh chestnuts, skinned
4 cups chicken stock
1/2 cup butter
2 medium onions, chopped
6 stalks celery, diced

salt and pepper to taste
2 tbs. butter
1 tbs. flour
1 cup light cream

Place chestnuts in the slow cooker and cover with stock and 1/4 cup of the butter. Set on low heat and cook for 3 to 4 hours or until chestnuts are soft. Strain off chestnuts; reserve liquid and puree softened chestnuts with a food processor or blender until smooth. Add a little liquid, if needed, to make mixture smooth. In a heavy saucepan, melt remaining butter and add onions. Cover and cook until soft but not brown. Stir in chestnut puree and add remaining stock and celery. Season to taste with salt and pepper. Knead butter and flour together and add to soup, stirring until thickened. Strain soup; add cream; heat just to a boil. Retaste for seasoning. Serve with croutons.

BEST EVER CHICKEN STOCK

Chicken stock is the basis for many soups and sauces, and can be used in place of butter or oil to add flavor without fat when frying vegetables. Adding onion skins to the stock will give it extra flavor and a darker color.

2 lb. chicken parts
1 lb. veal bones
1 gal. cold water
4 carrots, diced
2 medium onions, diced
1/2 tsp. whole cloves
3 stalks celery, diced
1 tbs. salt

1 tsp. black peppercorns
handful fresh parsley stems, not leaves
2 bay leaves
1 fresh rosemary sprig, or 1 tsp. dried whole
1 fresh thyme sprig, or 1 tsp. dried
few blades mace, or dash nutmeg
2 cloves garlic, peeled and left whole

Place chicken parts and veal bones in the slow cooker and cover with water. Set slow cooker on high heat and as scum rises to top, remove it with a slotted spoon. After scum ceases to form, set slow cooker on low heat and add remaining ingredients. If fresh rosemary and thyme are not available, wrap dried whole rosemary and thyme in cheesecloth; place in pot and remove at end of cooking. Cook for 6 hours; strain broth; taste and adjust seasonings. When cool, refrigerate until ready to use.

CREAM OF CHICKEN SOUP

Servings: 8

Once you have a great stock, you can quickly make a cream of chicken soup. If you wish, pour a little cream into the center of each serving.

4 cups chicken stock
2 cups chopped celery
2 cloves garlic, minced
3/4 cup half-and-half
salt and white pepper to taste
2 cups minced cooked chicken
1/2 cup grated Parmesan cheese

Put stock, celery and garlic in the slow cooker. Set on high heat and cook until celery is tender, about 30 minutes. Pour mixture into a food processor workbowl or blender container and puree until smooth. Return pureed mixture to pot and set cooker on low heat. Add remaining ingredients and stir until heated through and cheese has melted.

SPANISH PORK AND BEAN SOUP

Servings: 10-12

This is definitely a main course soup, hearty with beans, Spanish sausage and smoked ham. Serve it with a tossed salad and cornbread or tortillas.

1/4 lb. dried chickpeas
1/4 lb. dried navy beans
1/4 lb. salt pork or bacon, diced
1/4 lb. Spanish sausage (chorizo) or
   garlic sausage
1/4 lb. smoked ham, diced
2 qt. beef stock
3 cloves garlic, minced

1 ham bone
2 tomatoes, chopped
1 1/2 tsp. ground cumin
4-5 potatoes, peeled and diced
salt and pepper to taste
1/2 lb. fresh spinach, well washed
3 tbs. butter

Rinse chickpeas and navy beans; cover with water and soak overnight. Drain and discard water. In a skillet, cook pork until browned. Remove pork and cook sausage until no pink is visible. Discard fat. Cut sausage into slices and set aside with salt pork and ham. Place peas and beans in the slow cooker with stock, garlic, ham bone, tomatoes, cumin, potatoes, salt and pepper. Cook on low heat for 8 to 9 hours or until chickpeas are tender. In skillet, sauté spinach in butter until all liquid is evaporated. Add cooked spinach and reserved meats to soup. Taste and adjust seasonings.

BEEF VEGETABLE BARLEY SOUP

This easy recipe has an unusual ingredient, oatmeal, that gives it body and a special flavor.

1 lb. beef stew meat, in 1-inch cubes
1 large beef knuckle bone, cut in half
1 large onion, diced
3 stalks celery, coarsely chopped
2 cloves garlic, peeled and left whole
1 tsp. salt
1 medium rutabaga, peeled and
  cut into cubes

3 qt. water
8 carrots, cut into 1-inch pieces
2 parsnips, peeled and cut into
  $1/2$-inch pieces
3 beef bouillon cubes
1 cup barley
$1/2$ cup oatmeal
salt and pepper to taste

Place stew meat, knuckle bone, onion, celery, garlic, salt, rutabaga and water in the slow cooker. Set on low heat and cook for 7 to 8 hours. Remove knuckle bone and strip off any meat and marrow. Discard bone. Add meat and marrow to slow cooker. Add carrots, parsnips and bouillon cubes and cook on low heat for 2 hours. Add barley and oatmeal and cook for 1 to 2 hours. Taste and add salt and pepper, if desired. Soup is done when vegetables are tender.

CHICKPEA SOUP

Make this hearty soup from chickpeas, sausage, cabbage and a pinch of saffron.

1 lb. dried chickpeas
3 qt. chicken or beef stock
1 ham bone
pinch saffron
2-3 bay leaves
4 cloves garlic, minced
2 medium onions, chopped
2 cups potatoes, peeled and diced
1-2 cooked Spanish sausage (chorizo), sliced
3 cups finely chopped cabbage
salt and pepper to taste

Soak chickpeas in water overnight; drain and discard water. Place chickpeas in the slow cooker with stock, ham bone, saffron, bay leaves, garlic and onions. Set cooker on low heat and cook for 8 hours. Add potatoes, sausage, cabbage, salt and pepper and cook for 2 hours longer or until potatoes are done. Remove ham bone; remove any meat from bone; discard bone and add ham back to pot. Taste and adjust seasonings.

VICHYSSOISE

This is a classic leek and potato soup that has been adapted to the slow cooker. Traditionally this soup is served cold, but it can be served hot.

2 lb. leeks
2 lb. potatoes
7 cups chicken stock
$2\frac{1}{4}$ cups milk
$1\frac{1}{2}$ cups cream
salt and white pepper to taste
fresh chopped chives for garnish

Trim off tough green leaves from leeks; split bulbs open and carefully wash out dirt between layers. Thinly slice leeks. Peel potatoes and dice. Place leeks, potatoes and chicken stock in the slow cooker; set on low heat and cook for 3 to 4 hours or until vegetables are tender. Puree entire mixture with a food processor or blender. Return mixture to slow cooker and add milk, cream, salt and white pepper. Cook on low heat until mixture is heated through. Taste and adjust seasoning. If serving chilled, allow soup to come to room temperature and then refrigerate. Garnish with chopped fresh chives.

LENTIL SOUP

Lentils are high in protein and full of fiber. This soup is better the second day. If served with a side dish of rice, you have a meal high in protein.

2 tbs. butter
1/2-3/4 cup diced onion
2-3 cloves garlic, minced
1 1/2 cups dried lentils
4 cups water
2 cups tomato juice
1 tsp. salt, or more to taste
2 bay leaves
pinch dill seed, optional

Set the slow cooker on high heat and melt butter in pot. Add onion and garlic and sauté until tender. Set cooker on low heat. Rinse lentils well and drain. Add lentils and water and cook on low for 4 to 5 hours. Add tomato juice, salt, bay leaves and dill seed, if desired, and cook an additional 3 hours. Taste and adjust seasonings. Remove bay leaves before serving.

LAMB AND BEAN SOUP

This is a delicious, hearty soup.

3/4 cup dried white beans
3/4 cup dried kidney beans
2 lb. lamb shanks
2 onions, sliced
3 leeks, sliced
1 turnip, peeled and diced
1/2 cup shredded cabbage
3 tomatoes, peeled, seeded and
    coarsely chopped
1 cup chopped mixed green and
    red bell peppers

1/4 cup sliced mushrooms
3 tbs. finely chopped celery
6 cloves garlic, minced
3 bay leaves
1 tsp. dried summer savory
1 tsp. salt, or to taste
1/4 tsp. pepper
1 cup red wine
2 1/2 qt. water
chopped fresh parsley and grated
    Parmesan cheese for garnish

In the slow cooker, place all beans; cover with water and soak overnight. Drain and discard water. Add remaining ingredients except garnish. Set cooker on low heat for 10 to 12 hours. Occasionally skim off fat that forms on surface. Remove bay leaves and lamb shanks. Strip any remaining meat from bones; discard bones and add meat to soup. Taste and adjust seasonings. Garnish.

VEGETARIAN ENTRÉES AND SIDE DISHES

FALAFEL (CHICKPEA PATTIES)

Falafel is a Middle Eastern food made from chickpeas (garbanzo beans) that are formed into little patties and quickly fried. Serve them in pita bread with hummus and sprouts or tabbouleh salad, and, according to tradition, tahini (sesame paste).

$1/2$ lb. dried chickpeas or fava beans
water to cover
1 tbs. chopped cilantro
1 tbs. chopped fresh parsley
4 green onions, chopped
2 cloves garlic, minced

$1/2$-1 tsp. ground cumin
pinch baking soda
salt and pepper to taste
water to moisten, optional
olive oil for frying

Rinse dried beans under running water; place in the slow cooker and cover with water (at least 2 inches over top of beans). Cook on low heat for 8 to 10 hours. Pour off water; rinse under cold water and allow to drain. Place cooked beans in a food processor workbowl or blender container and puree until slightly grainy. Add cilantro, parsley, onions, garlic, cumin, soda, salt and pepper. Blend until just mixed. Taste mixture and adjust seasonings. Moisten your hands with water and form mixture into small patties. If mixture seems too dry to form proper patties, add a small amount of water. Heat olive oil in a skillet and fry patties until brown on both sides.

KAMUT VEGETABLE SALAD

Servings: 6-8

This healthy, chewy grain complements vegetables perfectly.

1 cup whole grain kamut
3 cups water
1/2 tsp. salt
1 cup chopped celery
1 cup chopped red cabbage

1/2 cup diced red bell peppers
1/4 cup diced green onions
1/4 cup diced red onion
2-4 tbs. chopped cilantro, to taste

Place kamut, water and salt in the slow cooker. Set on low heat and cook for 8 to 9 hours. Allow grains to cool thoroughly. Mix in celery, cabbage, peppers, red and green onions and cilantro. Add enough vinaigrette to moisten.

BALSAMIC VINAIGRETTE

1 cup olive oil
1/3 cup balsamic vinegar
1 tsp. Dijon mustard

1-2 tsp. sugar
salt and pepper to taste

Mix all ingredients together with a food processor or blender. Taste and add additional seasonings to personal taste.

MARINATED GARBANZO BEAN SALAD

Instead of the same old three-bean salad, try something new. This salad can be served warm or cold.

3 cups dried garbanzo beans
  (chickpeas)
water to cover
1 tbs. olive oil
2 tbs. vegetable or chicken stock

1/2 cup chopped onion
1 tbs. dried thyme
1/2 red bell pepper, chopped
1/2 cup dried currants or raisins
2 tbs. balsamic vinegar

In the slow cooker, cover dried beans with water (at least 2 inches above beans). Cook on low heat for 8 hours. Drain beans; discard water and measure out 3 cups. (If there are extra beans, add to a tossed salad or use to make *Hummus Dip*, page 13.) Place oil and 1 tbs. vegetable stock in a skillet. Add onion and thyme; cook on medium until onion is soft and beginning to turn brown, about 10 minutes. Add remaining 1 tbs. vegetable stock and pepper; stir-fry for several minutes. Add currants and cooked beans; cook for 5 minutes. Remove mixture from heat, pour into a bowl and cool. Add vinegar and mix well. Taste and add more seasonings or vinegar to taste.

LAYERED BLACK BEAN SALAD

This colorful, unique salad goes well with corn chips or a crusty bread. Display the layers in a straight-sided glass bowl.

BEAN MIXTURE
1 cup dried black beans
4 cups water
1/2 cup chopped green bell peppers
1/2 cup chopped red bell peppers
1/2 cup chopped yellow bell peppers
1/2 cup chopped onion
dash red pepper flakes

Rinse dried beans and place in the slow cooker. Cover with water; set cooker on low heat and cook for 8 to 9 hours. Remove beans from cooker; discard water and rinse beans. Cool. Mix beans with peppers, onion and pepper flakes; set aside.

DRESSING

1 cup balsamic red wine vinegar
3/4 cup olive oil
2-3 cloves garlic, peeled
1 tbs. sugar
salt to taste

Mix vinegar, olive oil, whole garlic cloves, sugar and salt in a saucepan. Simmer for 10 minutes. Cool and strain. Pour cooled dressing over bean mixture and allow flavors to blend for at least 2 hours or overnight, if time permits.

SALAD INGREDIENTS

sour cream, low-fat if available
bottled salsa
chopped lettuce
chopped green onions
chopped fresh parsley for garnish

The size of the bowl determines the quantity of salad ingredients. Place 1/2 of the bean mixture in bowl. Spread a thin layer of sour cream over beans and then a thin layer of salsa. Follow with a 1-inch-thick layer of chopped lettuce; sprinkle with chopped green onions and top with remaining bean mixture. Sprinkle with chopped parsley.

BLACK BEAN CHILI

This is ideal for cold, autumn or winter days. Black beans add great flavor and are low in fat. If served with rice or potatoes, this makes a healthy, complete protein meal.

1 cup dried black beans
4 cups water
1/2 tsp. cumin seeds
1/8 tsp. cayenne pepper
1/2 tsp. paprika
1 medium onion, chopped
3 cloves garlic, mashed
1 tsp. dry mustard
1 tsp. chili powder
2 large tomatoes, prefer plum variety
2 tbs. tomato paste
1/2 red bell pepper, chopped
1 can (4 oz.) diced green chiles
6 oz. low-fat cheese, shredded
salt to taste

Soak beans in water overnight. Drain and discard water. Place beans and fresh water in the slow cooker and set on high heat. Cook until tender, about 6 hours.

The next step is not necessary, but intensifies the flavor. Heat a skillet over medium heat and toast cumin seeds until they begin to pop, about 2 to 3 minutes. Add cayenne pepper and paprika and cook for 1 minute. (Note: This is very volatile, so have the fan running.)

To cooked beans in slow cooker, add toasted spices and onion. Mix mashed garlic with dry mustard and add to bean mixture. Add chili powder. Seed and chop tomatoes and add to pot with tomato paste, pepper and green chiles. Set cooker on low heat and cook for 3 to 4 hours. Before serving, add shredded cheese. Taste and add salt, if desired.

VARIATION: To make a dip or to use as a sandwich spread, omit the cheese and puree mixture with a food processor or blender.

SIMPLE TOMATO SAUCE

Servings: 6

Try this recipe for a quick, tasty sauce that takes just minutes to prepare. Serve over pasta or spaghetti squash with a sprinkling of Parmesan for a good vegetarian meal.

2 tbs. olive oil
1 large onion, chopped
4-5 cups canned plum tomatoes, undrained
1 can (6 oz.) tomato paste
2 tsp. dried basil, or 2 tbs. fresh chopped
2 tsp. dried oregano, or 2 tbs. fresh
2 tsp. sugar
salt and pepper to taste
1 cup sliced fresh mushrooms, optional

Set the slow cooker on high heat; add oil and onion. Allow onion to soften and wilt slightly. Set cooker on low heat, add remaining ingredients and cook for 4 to 6 hours. Taste and season to personal preference before serving.

LENTIL SPAGHETTI SAUCE

Spaghetti sauce is generally loved by all, but if you want to cut down on fat and meats, lentils are a good substitute. Serve over pasta, cooked, shredded spaghetti squash or rice.

1 tbs. olive oil
1 medium onion, chopped
2-3 cloves garlic, minced
2 cans (15 oz. each) tomato sauce
1 cup chopped fresh tomatoes
1 cup water
$\frac{1}{2}$ cup lentils

$\frac{1}{2}$ tsp. dried oregano
1 tsp. dried basil
$\frac{1}{2}$ tsp. salt
$\frac{1}{2}$ tsp. dried thyme
dash red pepper flakes, cayenne
    pepper or Tabasco Sauce, optional

Set the slow cooker on high heat. Add oil and when hot, sauté onion and garlic until wilted. Set cooker on low heat; add tomato sauce, fresh tomatoes and water. Wash lentils well and add to slow cooker with remaining ingredients. Cook for 6 to 7 hours.

PARMESAN POLENTA

Polenta is a delicious alternative to potatoes or rice. It is simple to fix and can be chilled in loaf form to serve sliced with Simple Tomato Sauce, *page 56, or the tomato sauce of your choice.*

2 cups polenta
6 cups boiling water
1 tsp. salt, or to taste
1/4 cup butter
1 cup grated Parmesan cheese,
  prefer Asiago

Place polenta in the slow cooker; pour boiling water on top and stir. Add remaining ingredients and stir. Set cooker on low heat and cook for 1 to 2 hours, stirring occasionally until mixture thickens and is smooth and soft.

If you wish to serve polenta with a sauce, butter a loaf pan; pour in hot polenta and refrigerate until firm. Cut solid polenta into slices, place on a platter, heat in the oven until warm and top with *Simple Tomato Sauce.*

JALAPEÑO GRITS

Grits can be quite plain, but with the addition of jalapeño cheese you get spectacular results. Use this as a starch in place of potatoes, rice or pasta — but be aware that this dish is very rich.

4 cups boiling water
1 cup dried corn grits
dash salt
1/2 cup butter
1 tube (8 oz.) jalapeño cheese, or 8 oz.
   pepper Jack cheese, grated
2 eggs, beaten
1 1/2 tsp. seasoning salt

In the slow cooker, pour boiling water over corn grits and stir until smooth. Set cooker on low heat and allow grits to sit in cooker for 5 to 10 minutes before adding remaining ingredients. Stir until butter melts. Cook for 3 to 4 hours. Taste and adjust seasoning.

MEAT ENTRÉES

MEXICAN POT ROAST

Servings: 8

Add a little flair to your standard pot roast by cooking it in a tomato-based sauce rich with garlic.

2 tbs. olive oil
1 beef pot roast, 4-5 lb.
salt and pepper to taste
1 medium onion, chopped
3 cloves garlic, minced
1 can (16 oz.) chopped tomatoes
2 bay leaves
$\frac{1}{2}$ tsp. dried thyme
1 cup fresh sliced mushrooms or canned mushrooms, optional

Heat olive oil in a skillet. Sprinkle roast with salt and pepper and brown well on all sides. Remove from skillet and set aside. Place remaining ingredients in the slow cooker and stir. Add browned roast; set cooker on low heat and cook for 8 to 10 hours. Roast is done when meat is tender enough to be cut with a fork.

Note: For a change of flavor, add 1 cup white wine at the beginning of cooking time.

BEER STEW

This is a basic beef stew with a twist — beer. It adds a unique flavor and helps tenderize the meat. If you like potatoes in your stew, add canned potatoes cut into chunks just before serving.

2 1/2 lb. beef stew meat or chuck roast
1 large onion, chopped
2 cloves garlic, minced
4-5 carrots, cut into chunks
2-3 stalks celery, sliced
16 oz. beer
2 1/2 tsp. salt

1/2 tsp. pepper
1 1/2 tsp. dried oregano
2 tbs. tomato paste
3-4 tbs. butter, melted
1/3 cup flour
chopped fresh parsley for garnish,
    optional

Cut beef into 1-inch squares. Place beef, onion, garlic, carrots, celery, beer, salt, pepper, oregano and tomato paste in the slow cooker. Set cooker on low heat and cook for 8 to 10 hours. Mix melted butter with flour until a smooth, thick paste (roux) is formed and stir into stew. Taste stew and adjust seasonings to your personal preference. Set slow cooker on high heat and allow mixture to thicken before serving. Garnish with chopped parsley.

CABBAGE ROLLS AND SAUERKRAUT

This is a fantastic recipe for cabbage rolls with a slightly sweet-and-sour, tomato-based sauce.

1 large cabbage
1 small onion, chopped
1 lb. lean ground beef
2 cloves garlic, minced
1 cup cooked rice
1 tbs. salt
1/2 tsp. pepper
3/4 tsp. dried thyme
1/2 tsp. paprika
1 jar (22 oz.) sauerkraut
1 jar (1 lb.) chopped tomatoes
3 tbs. lemon juice
3 tbs. brown sugar
1/4 cup vermouth
2 bay leaves
sour cream for garnish, optional

Remove cabbage core with a sharp knife. Parboil cabbage, core cavity-side down, for about 5 minutes to slightly wilt leaves and make them more pliable. Carefully separate leaves and cut out thickest part of stems with a small V cut to make leaves easier to wrap.

Mix onion, beef, garlic, rice, salt, pepper, thyme and paprika together in a bowl until well combined. Pour undrained sauerkraut into the slow cooker. Cup 1 cabbage leaf in your hand and fill with several spoonfuls of meat mixture. Wrap leaf around meat, fold in all all sides and secure with a wooden toothpick. Place on sauerkraut, seam-side down. Repeat until all meat mixture is used.

Prepare sauce: Mix together undrained tomatoes, lemon juice, brown sugar and vermouth; pour over cabbage rolls. Tuck bay leaves in juice where they can be easily removed later. Set cooker on low heat and cook for 10 to 12 hours. Serve cabbage rolls with sauce on top and a little sauerkraut. If desired, top with a dollop of sour cream.

SPECIAL BOLOGNESE SAUCE

The ingredients that make this sauce special are thyme and Dijon mustard, which aren't common Italian flavors! Give it a try — you'll be pleasantly surprised.

1 1/2 lb. lean ground beef
1 cup chopped onion
2 carrots, chopped
2 stalks celery, chopped
5 cups chopped, canned tomatoes
1 cup white wine
1 1/2 tsp. salt
1/2 tsp. pepper
4 cloves garlic, minced

2 tsp. dried oregano
2 tsp. dried basil
1 tsp. dried rosemary
1/2 tsp. anise seeds
1 tbs. dried thyme
1 1/2 tbs. Dijon mustard
1 tbs. sugar, or to taste
cooked pasta

In a skillet, brown beef and onion until no red remains in meat and beef is crumbled. Drain off excess fat. Place browned beef and onion in the slow cooker and stir in remaining ingredients. Cover and set cooker on low heat for 6 to 8 hours. Taste and adjust seasonings. Serve over hot pasta.

SOUTH AMERICAN BRAISED BEEF

Slow cooking can turn even a round steak into a fork-tender piece of meat. You can shred the meat and, with a little sauce, use it to fill tortillas.

2 cloves garlic, minced
2 lb. beef round steak
1 tsp. salt
1/4 tsp. pepper
2 tbs. lime or lemon juice
1 medium onion, chopped
1 cup chopped carrots
1 tsp. dried marjoram
1/2 cup beef broth
1 can (14 1/2 oz.) peeled tomatoes

Spread minced garlic on round steak and sprinkle with salt, pepper and lime juice. Place in the slow cooker and add remaining ingredients. Set cooker on low heat and cook for about 8 hours. Meat should be fork-tender and shred easily. If not, return to pot and cook for additional time. Taste and add extra seasonings if desired.

PICADILLO

Picadillo is a spicy, pickled-type meat mixture that is very popular in Mexico. It can be used in burritos, tacos, turnovers, empanadas or stuffed into chiles rellenos.

3 lb. boneless pork, cut into large cubes
1/2 large onion, sliced
3 cloves garlic, peeled and left whole
1 tbs. salt
water to cover meat
1/4 cup butter
1/2 large onion, finely chopped
3 cloves garlic, minced

8 peppercorns
5 whole cloves
1/2-inch stick cinnamon
1/4 cup raisins
2 tbs. slivered almonds
2-3 tbs. chopped candied fruit
2 tsp. salt, or to taste
1 1/2 lb. tomatoes, peeled and seeded

Place meat in the slow cooker. Add onion, garlic and salt. Cover mixture with water and cook on low heat for 8 to 10 hours. Strain meat; cool and shred or cut into small cubes. Heat butter in a skillet and sauté onion and minced garlic over medium heat until soft but not brown. Add meat and cook until it begins to brown. Crush peppercorns, cloves and cinnamon with a mortar and pestle or electric seed grinder and add to meat mixture. Gently stir in remaining ingredients, except tomatoes. Mash tomatoes slightly and add to meat mixture. Cook over high heat in skillet, stirring occasionally until moisture in mixture is evaporated. Taste and adjust seasonings.

COLORADO CHILI

This chili is made with large red Colorado chile peppers which are ground into a paste and added to cooked meat. Beans make a great accompaniment.

2 lb. leaf beef or pork
2 cups water
salt to taste
8 large dried red Colorado chile
    peppers
warm water to cover chili peppers

2 cloves garlic, peeled
1 tsp. dried oregano
1/4 cup vegetable oil, or less if desired
2 tbs. flour
salt to taste
pinch ground cumin, or to taste

Cut beef or pork into cubes and place in the slow cooker with water and salt. Cook on high heat for 1 to 2 hours. Drain meat and reserve liquid. While meat is cooking, cover peppers with warm water and soak for 20 to 30 minutes. Drain peppers and reserve liquid. Cut peppers open and remove seeds. Puree peppers, garlic and oregano with a food processor or blender to consistency of paste. To paste, add 1 cup reserved meat liquid and 1/2 cup reserved chile pepper liquid. Stir until well mixed. In a skillet, heat oil; stir in flour and add chile mixture, salt and cumin. Add chile mixture to slow cooker with meat and set on low heat. Cook for 4 to 6 hours. Taste and adjust seasonings.

INCREDIBLE CHILI

Servings: 12

This is the true chili made the old-fashioned way. It's worth the effort.

½ lb. bacon, diced
3 medium onions, minced
1½ lb. pork loin
1½ lb. sirloin tip
1½ lb. ground chuck (chili grind)
2 cans (15 oz. each) tomato sauce
18 oz. beer
3 cloves garlic, minced

1 jalapeño pepper, seeded and minced
2 tbs. ground cumin
½ tsp. dried oregano
2-3 tbs. mild chili powder
salt and pepper to taste
2 cups dried pinto beans, optional
grated cheese, optional

In a skillet, cook bacon until brown. Drain and place in the slow cooker. Remove all but a small amount of fat from skillet and sauté onions until slightly brown. Place onions in slow cooker. Cut pork loin and sirloin tip into ¼-inch dice and brown with ground chuck in skillet. Drain off fat and add meat to slow cooker. Add remaining ingredients except cheese. If you choose to use pinto beans, soak in water overnight, discard water, add beans to slow cooker and stir. Set cooker on low heat and cook for 6 to 8 hours. Meat should be very tender. Taste and adjust seasonings. If desired, sprinkle with cheese before serving.

OLIVE SPAGHETTI SAUCE

Servings: 8-10

When the old red spaghetti sauce gets boring, try something new. This sauce is made with green olives, but, if you don't like them, you can substitute black olives.

1 lb. lean ground beef
1/2 lb. ground veal
1/4 lb. Italian sausage
1 cup water
1 tsp. salt
1/8 tsp. pepper
1 can (28 oz.) tomatoes, chopped
12 oz. tomato paste
1 1/2 cups Burgundy wine
1 cup chopped onion

3/4 cup chopped green bell pepper
3 cloves garlic, crushed
2 tsp. sugar
1/2 tsp. chili powder
1 1/2 tsp. Worcestershire sauce
3 bay leaves
1 cup sliced mushrooms, fresh or canned
1/2 cup sliced stuffed green olives
grated Parmesan cheese

In a heavy skillet, brown beef, veal and sausage. Drain off fat. Put browned meat, water, salt, pepper, tomatoes, tomato paste, Burgundy, onion, peppers, garlic, sugar, chili powder, Worcestershire sauce, bay leaves and fresh mushrooms (not canned) in the slow cooker. Cook on low heat for 8 hours. About half an hour before serving, add olives to cooker. Add canned mushrooms if you are using them. Cook for 30 minutes longer. Remove bay leaves. Serve over pasta and sprinkle with Parmesan.

COUNTRY RIBS

What makes ribs really good is tender, succulent, drop-off-the-bone meat smothered in a delicious sauce. Here is the basic recipe for the ribs and several sauces — sauerkraut, barbecue, and Hawaiian — that complement the meat.

4-6 lb. country-style pork or beef ribs
water to cover meat
1 large onion, chopped
3 bay leaves

1 tbs. salt
1 tsp. peppercorns
2 tbs. cider vinegar
1 cup chopped celery

Place ribs in the slow cooker and cover with water. Add remaining ingredients. Set cooker on low heat and cook for 8 to 12 hours, depending on size of rib and type of meat used. Meat should be very tender. Skim top off broth and remove meat. Smother cooked meat in sauce of choice and place under a broiler to brown or on a grill.

KRAUT FOR RIBS

1 jar (32 oz.) sauerkraut
1 tsp. caraway seeds

pepper to taste, optional
chopped parsley for garnish

Heat sauerkraut, caraway seeds and pepper in a saucepan until hot. Place ribs on a platter and cover with flavored sauerkraut. Sprinkle with parsley and serve.

BARBECUE SAUCE FOR RIBS

1/4 cup butter
2 large onions, chopped
12 oz. tomato paste
3 cloves garlic, minced
1/4 cup Worcestershire sauce
1/4 cup cider vinegar

1/2 cup brown sugar, packed
1/2 cup sweet pickle relish
1/2 cup red or white wine
2 tsp. salt
2 tsp. dry mustard
few drops Liquid Smoke, optional

Heat butter in a heavy saucepan and sauté onions until tender. Add remaining ingredients. Add a few drops of Liquid Smoke, if desired. Cook on low heat for about half an hour. Taste and adjust seasonings.

HAWAIIAN SAUCE FOR RIBS

1/2 cup brown sugar, packed
1/2 cup cider vinegar
1 tsp. Worcestershire sauce
1/4 cup bottled chili sauce
2 tbs. soy sauce

2/3 cup ketchup
2 cups tidbits or crushed pineapple,
    drained, 1/4 cup juice reserved
1/4 cup cornstarch

Place sugar, vinegar, Worcestershire sauce, chili sauce, soy sauce and ketchup in a heavy saucepan over medium heat. Mix reserved pineapple with cornstarch to form a paste and add to heated mixture. Stir until thickened. Add drained pineapple. Taste and adjust seasonings.

SURPRISE SPARERIBS

The ribs are cooked slowly, marinated and finally barbecued or broiled. The surprise ingredient, Coca Cola, is added to the final basting sauce.

6 lb. pork spareribs
water to cover meat
4 tsp. pickling spices
1 tsp. salt
1½ cups brown sugar, packed
2 tbs. dry mustard
½ cup ketchup
½ cup Coca Cola

Cut ribs apart, place in the slow cooker and cover with water. Add pickling spices and salt. Cook on low heat for 6 hours or until ribs are tender. Discard liquid and place ribs in a shallow pan. Mix brown sugar and dry mustard together and sprinkle over ribs. Cover and refrigerate overnight. Mix ketchup and Coca Cola together and spread on ribs. Grill or broil until ribs are browned.

BURGUNDY BEEF

Whenever you cook with wine, use a wine you would gladly drink and you'll reap the rewards. Serve this with gnocchi, noodles, rice or potatoes.

1/4 cup butter
1/4 cup olive oil
1 can (1 1/4 lb.) small white onions
4 lb. chuck, cut into 2-inch cubes
1/4 cup flour
1 tsp. Kitchen Bouquet
1 tbs. tomato paste
3 cups Burgundy wine

1/4 tsp. pepper
3 bay leaves
1/2 tsp. dried thyme
1/2 tsp. dried marjoram
1 tbs. chopped fresh parsley
3/4 lb. fresh or canned mushrooms
chopped fresh parsley for garnish

In a skillet, heat butter and oil; sauté onions until brown. Remove from skillet and place in the slow cooker. In same skillet, brown meat cubes on all sides; add to slow cooker. Discard all but 1 tbs. fat from skillet. Add flour, Kitchen Bouquet and tomato paste to skillet; stir until smooth. Gradually stir in Burgundy wine. Add mixture to slow cooker with pepper, bay leaves, thyme, marjoram, parsley and mushrooms. Set cooker on low heat and cook for 8 to 9 hours. Taste and add salt, if desired. Remove bay leaves before serving. Garnish with a sprinkling of parsley.

BEEF IN BEER

This is a simple-to-fix onion and beef stew that goes well with mashed potatoes, noodles or rice.

3 lb. boneless beef chuck
2 tbs. flour
1 1/2 tsp. salt
1/8 tsp. pepper
1/2 tsp. crushed rosemary
2 tbs. vegetable oil
4 medium onions, sliced into rounds

2 cloves garlic, minced
2 bay leaves
4 whole cloves
1 can (12 oz.) beer
2 tbs. red wine vinegar
1 tsp. Dijon mustard
chopped fresh parsley for garnish

Trim fat from beef and cut into 1-inch cubes. Mix flour, salt, pepper and rosemary together and coat beef cubes. In a skillet, cook beef in oil until brown on all sides. Place beef in the slow cooker; cover with onions, garlic, bay leaves, cloves and beer. Cook on low heat for 8 to 9 hours or until beef is very tender. Before serving, remove bay leaves and stir in vinegar and mustard. Taste and adjust seasonings. Sprinkle with finely chopped parsley and serve.

SWEET AND SOUR BEEF

Sweet and sour is a popular flavor usually reserved for pork or chicken. This is a delicious beef version that is good served over rice or noodles.

2 lb. boneless chuck
1/3 cup flour
1 tsp. salt
1/4 tsp. black pepper
1 tbs. butter
1 tbs. olive oil
1 large onion, chopped
1/2 cup ketchup

1/4 cup brown sugar
1/4 cup red wine vinegar
1 tbs. Worcestershire sauce
1 cup water
1 tsp. salt
pepper to taste, optional
4-6 carrots, cut into matchstick strips

Cut beef into 1-inch cubes. Mix together flour, salt and pepper and dredge cubes in mixture. In a skillet, heat butter and olive oil and brown beef cubes. Place browned beef in the slow cooker and set on low heat . Add remaining ingredients except carrots. Cook for 8 to 9 hours or until meat is tender. Add carrots and cook for 1 1/2 to 2 hours longer. Taste, adjust seasonings and serve.

ORANGE MADEIRA POT ROAST

Servings: 6

This pot roast is marinated in a spicy orange sauce, cooked with the marinade and finished with a thickened sauce in which Madeira is added. Serve with rice or mashed potatoes.

1 can (6 oz.) frozen orange juice
concentrate
1/2 cup orange juice
1 tbs. grated orange zest
2 small onions, chopped
1 1/2 tsp. salt
1/2 tsp. pepper
1/2 tsp. ground cloves
1 1/4 tsp. ground coriander

1/4 tsp. ground cumin
3 1/2 lb. chuck roast
1 tbs. olive oil
1 tbs. butter
2 tbs. cornstarch
1/4 cup water
2 oranges, sliced
1/2 cup Madeira wine
chopped parsley for garnish, optional

In a bowl, mix together undiluted orange juice concentrate, orange juice, orange peel, onions, salt, pepper, cloves, coriander and cumin. Pour mixture over chuck roast and marinate for at least 6 hours in the refrigerator. Remove meat from marinade; scrape off excess liquid and reserve.

Heat oil and butter in a skillet on high heat and brown meat on both sides. Transfer meat to the slow cooker and pour reserved marinade on top. Set cooker on low heat for 8 to 10 hours or until tender. Remove meat to a platter and keep warm until sauce is ready.

Mix cornstarch with water and pour into slow cooker. Stir as mixture thickens. Add orange slices and Madeira and simmer for 15 minutes. Taste and adjust seasonings. Slice meat; remove orange slices from pot and arrange around meat. Pour sauce over meat. If desired, garnish with a sprinkling of chopped parsley.

SAUSAGE AND BAKED BEANS

Servings: 9

Even though this recipe uses canned beans, adding delicious ingredients and cooking on low for a long time really enhances the flavor.

1 lb. ground pork sausage
4-5 slices bacon, diced
1 large onion, chopped
1 stalk celery, chopped
1 can (28 oz.) baked beans
3/4 tsp. dried basil
1 tbs. chopped fresh parsley

2 tbs. chutney
2 tbs. soy sauce
2 tbs. cider or red wine vinegar
1 can (15 oz.) tomatoes
1 tsp. salt
1/2 cup molasses

Brown sausage and bacon in a skillet and drain off fat. Place browned meats in the slow cooker with remaining ingredients. Set cooker on low heat and cook for 6 hours. Check the quantity of liquid; if it seems excessive, pour a little off and reserve for later. Stir and continue cooking an additional 6 hours. Check to determine if you need to add some reserved liquid. Taste and adjust seasonings.

WINE STEW

Stew does not have to be limited to carrots and potatoes in gravy. Try something new — mix the meats, use wine and serve with rice.

2 tbs. butter or bacon fat
2½ lb. top sirloin, cut into 2-inch pieces
½ lb. ham, prefer Westphalian
2 large onions, diced
½ cup stuffed green olives, halved
2-3 cloves garlic, minced
¾ tsp. dried thyme
½ cup raisins

3 cups red wine
2 tsp. pepper
1 tsp. salt, or to taste
¼ cup brandy
¾ cup cream
¼ cup flour
½ cup water

In a skillet, heat butter on high heat and brown beef cubes. Add ham and onions; stir until slightly brown. Transfer mixture to the slow cooker and set on low heat. Add olives, garlic, thyme, raisins and wine. Cook for 7 to 8 hours. Add pepper, salt, brandy and cream; cook for 1 hour longer. Remove meat from cooker and keep warm. Turn cooker on high; mix flour with water and add to cooker. Stir until mixture begins to thicken. If you desire a thicker sauce, add more flour-water mixture. Taste and adjust seasonings. Pour sauce over meat and serve.

SWEET AND SOUR LAMB CHOPS

An unusual sauce, made with crème de menthe liqueur, is served over broiled or sautéed lamb chops.

2 cups thinly sliced onions
1/4 cup butter
1/2 cup crème de menthe
1/2 cup cider or red wine vinegar
2 tbs. sugar
4 tsp. lemon juice
1 cup beef broth
1 tsp. dried rosemary
6-12 lamb chops, depending on size

Place onions and butter in the slow cooker; set on low heat and cook for 2 to 3 hours. Add crème de menthe, vinegar, sugar and lemon juice; stir and cook until mixture looks syrupy, about 30 minutes. Stir in beef broth and rosemary and simmer on low for 45 minutes to 1 hour. Taste and adjust seasoning. Keep sauce warm in slow cooker while broiling or sautéing chops. Pour sauce over lamb chops and serve.

GROUND LAMB AND ONION CURRY

This is a great dish to have when you crave something spicy and different. If ground lamb is not available, you can substitute ground beef.

3 tbs. vegetable oil
2 large onions, thinly sliced
1 tbs. peeled, chopped fresh ginger
2 cloves garlic, minced
1 tsp. salt
1 lb. ground lamb
2-3 tsp. curry powder
1/4 tsp. cinnamon
1/2 tsp. dried turmeric

1/2 tsp. ground coriander
1/2 tsp. ground cumin
dash Tabasco Sauce or red pepper flakes
pepper to taste
4 cups chopped peeled, seeded tomatoes
2 tbs. plain yogurt
cooked rice
chopped cilantro for garnish

Heat oil in a skillet and add onions, ginger, garlic and salt. Sauté until onions begin to brown. Add lamb and cook until no longer pink. Drain fat from mixture. Add curry powder, cinnamon, turmeric, coriander, cumin, Tabasco and pepper. Stir for several minutes to release flavor of spices. Transfer ingredients to the slow cooker and set on low heat for 1 to 2 hours. Add tomatoes and yogurt to lamb mixture and cook for 30 minutes more. Taste and adjust seasonings. Serve over rice and garnish liberally with chopped cilantro.

PORK ADOBO

This is a braised pork dish common in the Philippines. Serve with white rice or more healthful brown rice.

2 1/2 lb. lean pork
salt to taste
1/4 cup flour
1 tbs. vegetable oil
2-3 cloves garlic, minced
2 medium onions, quartered
2 bay leaves

1/4 cup cider vinegar
1 tbs. soy sauce
1/4 cup water
1 tsp. sugar, optional
beaten fried egg for garnish, cut into
thin strips, optional

Remove fat from pork and cut into 1 1/2-inch cubes. Mix salt and flour together and coat pork cubes. Heat oil in a skillet and cook pork until brown. Add garlic and cook for 1 minute. Add onions and bay leaves and cook until onions begin to brown. Transfer ingredients to the slow cooker. Set cooker on low heat; add remaining ingredients, except sugar and egg. Cook for 6 to 8 hours or until pork is tender. Taste and adjust seasonings. Add sugar, if desired. Remove bay leaves. Garnish with thin strips of fried beaten egg, if desired.

POULTRY ENTRÉES

CHICKEN CURRY

Ideally, curries should be accompanied with several condiments like chutney, chopped green onions, raisins, chopped nuts, etc. Serve with rice.

6 whole chicken breasts
water to cover chicken
1/2 tsp. peppercorns
1 tsp. salt
2 stalks celery, chopped
1/2 cup butter
1 tbs. vegetable oil
2 medium onions, chopped
3 cloves garlic, minced
2 stalks celery, chopped
3 tbs. chopped fresh parsley
1 cucumber, chopped, prefer English
   variety

2 apples, cored, peeled and chopped
1/4 cup flour
1 tsp. nutmeg
1 tsp. dry mustard
3 tbs. curry powder, or to taste
2 cups chicken broth
2 cups cream
1 cup coconut milk
1 1/2 tsp. salt
1 tbs. lemon juice

Split chicken breasts and place in the slow cooker. Add water, peppercorns, salt and celery. Set on low heat and cook for 5 to 6 hours or until chicken is tender. Remove chicken; discard liquid; debone chicken and cut meat into dice or shred. Set aside. Turn slow cooker on high; heat butter and oil; add onions, garlic, celery, parsley, cucumber and apples. Sauté until tender, stirring frequently. Stir in flour, nutmeg, mustard and curry powder; cook for 5 minutes longer. Add chicken broth, cream, coconut milk and salt. Allow mixture to heat up; set cooker on low heat and cook sauce for 2 to 3 hours. Press sauce through a sieve to make smooth. Add lemon juice; taste and adjust seasonings. Transfer chicken to slow cooker and cover with sauce. Leave on low heat until ready to serve.

CHICKEN EN MOLE

Servings: 8

Mole is a Mexican reddish-brown sauce that has an unusual ingredient, chocolate. The traditional recipe uses finely chopped roasted peanuts, but here it is modernized with peanut butter.

4 cups canned chopped tomatoes
1 large onion, chopped
2 cloves garlic, minced
3/4 cup peanut butter
1/4 cup tahini, or ground sesame seeds
2 tbs. sugar
1 1/2-2 tbs. chili powder
1/2 tsp. anise
1/2 tsp. cinnamon
1/2 tsp. ground cloves
1/2 tsp. ground coriander

1/2-l tsp. ground cumin
2 cups chicken stock
salt and pepper to taste
2 squares (2 oz.) unsweetened
   chocolate, grated
2 stewing chickens
water to cover chickens
1 tsp. salt
1 tsp. peppercorns
1 tbs. dried onion flakes, or 1/4 cup
   chopped onion
1 cup chopped celery

Place tomatoes, onion, garlic, peanut butter, tahini, sugar, chili powder, anise, cinnamon, cloves, coriander, cumin, chicken stock, salt and pepper in the slow cooker. Stir, cover, set on low heat and cook for 6 to 8 hours. Add grated chocolate. Taste and adjust seasonings to your preference. You may need to add additional sugar to make mixture slightly sweet.

Cut chicken into pieces and remove skin. Place in a pan and cover with water. Add salt, peppercorns, onion flakes and celery and bring to a boil. Reduce heat; simmer until chicken is tender, 35 to 45 minutes. Remove from heat; separate meat from bone or serve as poached chicken pieces. Cover with mole sauce.

CRANBERRY CHICKEN

Servings: 4

Cranberries add a slightly tangy flavor to slow-cooked chicken dishes. The berries tend to dissolve so they are not noticeable. With the addition of a little brown sugar, the chicken takes on a slightly sweet-and-sour taste. This dish is good served with brown rice.

1 boiler chicken
3/4 cup chopped onion
1 cup fresh or frozen cranberries
1 tsp. salt
1/4 tsp. cinnamon
1/4 tsp. ground ginger

1 tsp. grated orange zest
1 cup orange juice
3 tbs. butter, melted
3 tbs. flour
2-3 tbs. brown sugar, optional

Cut chicken into quarters and remove skin. Place in the slow cooker with onion, cranberries, salt, cinnamon, ginger, orange zest and orange juice. Cover and cook on low heat for 5 to 6 hours. Remove chicken from pot and separate meat from bone; set aside. Mix butter and flour together to form a thick paste. Stir paste into liquid in pot and set on high heat to thicken sauce. Add chicken meat and taste. Add brown sugar and any additional seasonings to suit your taste.

CHUTNEY CHICKEN SALAD

Servings: 6

Poaching chicken slowly gives it a succulent quality perfect for salads.

4-5 full chicken breasts
2 bay leaves
1 tsp. salt
1/2 tsp. peppercorns
1/2 medium onion, coarsely chopped
2 stalks celery, chopped
water to cover
1 cup mayonnaise
1/2 cup chopped chutney

1 tsp. curry powder
2 tsp. grated lemon or lime zest
1/4 cup lemon or lime juice
1/2 tsp. salt
1 1/2 cups canned pineapple chunks
1/2 cup sliced green onions
1 1/2 cups chopped celery
1/2 cup slivered toasted almonds

Cut chicken breasts in half and place in the slow cooker with bay leaves, salt, peppercorns, onion and celery. Cover with water. Set cooker on low and cook for 4 to 6 hours. Take out a chicken piece and cut it in half to make sure chicken is cooked thoroughly. Remove chicken from pot and cool. If you wish, strain vegetables from liquid and save for future use. Dice chicken to make about 4 cups chicken meat. Combine mayonnaise, chutney, curry, lemon peel, lemon juice and salt. Toss with chicken; add remaining ingredients, except almonds. Chill well. When ready to serve, sprinkle with almonds.

CHICKEN PASTA SALAD

Pasta and succulent poached chicken are perfect companions.

3 whole chicken breasts
water to cover
1 stalk celery, chopped
1/2 medium onion, chopped
1/2 tsp. salt
a few peppercorns
6 oz. dried pasta of choice
1/2 cup vegetable oil
1 tbs. sesame oil

1/3 cup light soy sauce
1/3 cup rice vinegar
3 tbs. sugar
1/4 tsp. pepper
1/2 tsp. ground ginger
1/4 cup chopped fresh parsley
1/3 cup sliced green onions
6 cups fresh spinach, well washed
1/4 cup toasted sesame seeds

Cut chicken breasts in half and place in the slow cooker. Cover with water and add celery, onion, salt and peppercorns. Set on low heat and cook for 5 to 6 hours. When chicken is cooked thoroughly; remove and cool. Cut into chunks or shred. Cook dried pasta according to package directions until just barely tender *(al dente);* drain and set aside to cool. In a separate bowl, combine oils, soy sauce, vinegar, sugar, pepper and ginger; mix well. Add to chicken and pasta and marinate together for at least 1 hour. Toss with parsley, onions, spinach and sesame seeds. Taste and adjust seasonings before serving.

NECTARINE CHICKEN

Here is another new and unique chicken dish. It is simple to prepare and very low in fat. Serve it with brown rice.

1 chicken, 3½ lb.
4-6 nectarines
1 tsp. salt
¼ cup brown sugar, packed
1½ tsp. ground ginger
½ tsp. nutmeg
pepper to taste
2 tbs. butter and 2 tbs. flour to thicken, optional

Cut chicken into pieces; remove skin and all visible fat and set aside. Leave peel on nectarines, remove pits and cut into slices. Place chicken in the slow cooker and add remaining ingredients, except butter and flour. Set on low heat and cook for 5 to 6 hours. Cooked chicken can be gently removed and kept on the bone or deboned and returned to pot. Taste and adjust seasonings. If you prefer thicker sauce, mix butter and flour together to form a paste; stir into hot mixture and thicken gradually. If you left chicken on bone, pour sauce over chicken to serve.

STUFFED CHICKEN ROLLS

This is a low-fat, easy meal that looks and tastes like you spent hours in the kitchen. Serve this with a rice pilaf or simple mashed potatoes.

3 whole chicken breasts, skinned,
  boned and cut in half
6 thin slices prosciutto or ham
6 thin slices low-fat Swiss cheese
flour to coat chicken
1/2 lb. sliced fresh mushrooms
1/2 cup chicken stock
1/2 cup white wine or Marsala wine

1/4 tsp. dried rosemary
1/4 cup grated Parmesan cheese
2 tsp. cornstarch
1 tbs. water
1 tsp. Kitchen Bouquet
salt and pepper to taste
1 tsp. sugar, optional

Place chicken pieces between 2 pieces of waxed paper and pound until slightly flattened. Place 1 slice prosciutto and 1 slice cheese on each breast and roll up. Secure with a toothpick and roll in flour. Put mushrooms in the slow cooker and place chicken rolls on top of mushrooms. In a separate bowl, mix chicken stock, wine and rosemary together and pour over chicken. Sprinkle with Parmesan. Set slow cooker on low heat and cook for 6 hours. Just before serving, mix cornstarch, water and Kitchen Bouquet together. Remove chicken; add cornstarch mixture and stir until thickened. Add salt, pepper and sugar, if desired. Pour sauce over chicken and serve.

TURKEY LOAF

With the emphasis on low-fat meats, ground turkey is a great substitute for ground beef. This recipe uses a unique combination of ingredients for a slightly tangy flavor. Find a pan or dish that fits in your slow cooker, or use a coffee can.

$2\frac{1}{2}$ lb. ground turkey
1 medium onion, chopped
2 eggs
$\frac{1}{3}$ cup milk
2 tbs. prepared horseradish
3 tbs. bottled chili sauce

1 cup breadcrumbs
1 tsp. salt
2 cloves garlic, minced
$\frac{1}{4}$ cup minced fresh parsley
sour cream for garnish, optional
capers for garnish, optional

Mix all ingredients except garnishes together. Cook a small amount of mixture in a skillet and taste. Adjust seasonings to your personal taste. Place mixture in a pan that fits into the slow cooker. Place a trivet in bottom of cooker and place pan on trivet. Set cooker on low heat and cook for 7 to 8 hours. Depending on shape of pan, cooking hours may vary. There should be no pink left in meat when done. Drain off any visible fat. If desired, add a thin layer of sour cream to the top and sprinkle with a few capers to serve.

SAUCES AND RELISHES

APPLE CRANBERRY RELISH

Here in the Pacific Northwest where apples grow in abundance, we add apples to recipes for sweetness and sometimes tartness. This recipe can be varied by adding spices like cinnamon, cloves, allspice and/or nutmeg to give it more of a chutney flavor.

8 cups apples, peeled and sliced
12 oz. fresh cranberries
1 cup boiling water
2 cups sugar
¼ cup cornstarch

Place apples, cranberries, boiling water and 1 cup of the sugar in the slow cooker, set on low heat and cook for 4 to 6 hours. Mix remaining 1 cup sugar and cornstarch together and stir into cranberry mixture. Cook until sugar is dissolved and juice is clear. Cool and refrigerate until ready to serve.

CRANBERRY CHUTNEY

Slow cookers are great for highly spiced fruit dishes like compotes and chutneys. Cranberry chutneys are best served with poultry and pork entrées and, of course, curry dishes.

4 cups fresh cranberries
1 cup water
½ cup golden raisins
½ cup dark raisins
2 cups sugar
1 tsp. ground ginger
1 tsp. cinnamon
½ tsp. ground allspice
pinch ground cloves
½ tsp. salt
1 can (20 oz.) crushed pineapple, drained

Place all ingredients in the slow cooker and stir. Set cooker on low heat and cook for 4 to 6 hours. Taste and adjust seasonings.

NECTARINE CHUTNEY

A fruit chutney like this goes well with Indian curries, as well as meat and fowl dishes. It can also be added to other sauces to bring out an unusual spiciness.

2½ lb. nectarines, peeled, pitted and sliced
1½ cups brown sugar, packed
1 cup cider vinegar
¼ cup diced crystallized ginger
1 tbs. salt, or to taste
¼ cup chopped onion
1 tsp. dry mustard
¼ tsp. cinnamon
⅛ tsp. ground cloves
½ cup slivered almonds, toasted

Place nectarines in the slow cooker with brown sugar, vinegar, ginger, salt, onion, mustard, cinnamon and cloves. Stir mixture well, set cooker on low heat and cook for 3 to 4 hours or until thick. Taste and adjust seasoning. Cool. Add almonds and refrigerate until ready to use. If desired, place mixture in a sterilized jar and process to heat seal.

PEACH PINEAPPLE CHUTNEY

Makes: 10 cups

Chutney is certainly becoming more popular, especially with increased interest in Indian cooking. This chutney goes well with wild game, lamb, curries, turkey, chicken, pork or even ham. Ginger already adds heat to your recipe, so be careful with the amount of cayenne.

5 cups peeled fruits: peaches, pineapple and apples
1 lemon, thinly sliced and seeded
2 cloves garlic, chopped
2¼ cups brown sugar, packed
¾ cup chopped crystallized ginger
2 tsp. salt
½ tsp. cayenne pepper, or more to taste
2 cups cider vinegar
1 cup mixed dark and light raisins

Mix any proportion of fruits and chop coarsely. Cut lemon slices into quarters and add to the slow cooker with fruits. Add remaining ingredients; set cooker on low heat and cook for 4 to 6 hours. Stir occasionally to prevent scorching. After cooling, keep refrigerated until ready to use. If you choose to can, process for 5 minutes in a water bath after ladling into sterile jars.

HEALTHY APPLE BUTTER

For health-minded people, this recipe is sugarless, salt-free and fat-free. What more could you ask?

8 lb. apples, peeled, cored and diced
1½ cups apple juice
2 tsp. cinnamon
1 tsp. nutmeg, or more to taste

Place apples in a blender container or food processor workbowl with apple juice and blend until smooth. Transfer to the slow cooker, set on low heat and cook for 6 to 7 hours. Stir occasionally. Let mixture cool; reblend and stir in spices. If desired, add more spices to taste. Store in the refrigerator after cooling to room temperature.

PEAR HONEY

Makes: 1 1/2-2 quarts

Pear honey is a spread something like apple butter that can be used on toast, crumpets, muffins, etc.

15 pears, peeled and cored
3 whole oranges
3 tbs. lemon juice
1 can (20 oz.) crushed pineapple
3-4 cups sugar, or more to taste

Use pears that are not overly ripe. Cut pears into chunks. Slice oranges, with peel left on, and remove seeds. With a food processor or blender, puree both fruits. Place all ingredients in the slow cooker and cook for 4 to 6 hours or until thick. Taste and add more sugar, if desired. Amount of sugar may vary considerably depending on ripeness of pears. Store in the refrigerator.

SPICED APPLESAUCE

Applesauce is becoming more popular as a substitute for high-sugar sauces and syrups. A favorite alternative is to use applesauce on pancakes in the place of syrup. You can play with the spices for more variety.

12 apples, peeled, cored and sliced
½ cup sugar, or more to taste
2 tbs. lemon juice
1 tsp. grated lemon zest
1 stick (4-6 inch) cinnamon*
½ tsp. nutmeg
¼ tsp. ground allspice
pinch ground cloves

Place all ingredients in the slow cooker and set on low heat. Cook for about 4 to 6 hours or until apples are tender. The time will vary depending on the type of apples used. Remove cinnamon stick. Taste and adjust seasonings. Serve warm or cold.

* A cinnamon stick doesn't darken the sauce as much, but you can substitute ½ tsp. cinnamon, or more, if you wish.

SWEET AND SOUR APRICOT SAUCE

This sauce is excellent for poultry, pork and lamb dishes or as an accompaniment to Chinese dishes. When apricots are plentiful, make a large batch and process for future use.

6 cups pitted, chopped apricots
1 cup light raisins
2 cups brown sugar, packed
1 tsp. cinnamon
1/2 tsp. ground cloves
1/2 tsp. ground allspice

2 tsp. salt
1/4-1/2 tsp. cayenne pepper, optional
2 large onions, chopped
4 cloves garlic, minced
24 oz. Japanese preserved ginger
1 1/2 cups cider vinegar

Place apricots, raisins, brown sugar, cinnamon, cloves, allspice, salt and cayenne, if desired, in the slow cooker and set on low heat. With a food processor or blender, puree onions, garlic, ginger and vinegar until smooth. Add onion mixture to slow cooker and stir. Cook for 3 to 4 hours, stirring occasionally, until mixture is thick like ketchup. Taste and adjust seasonings. Store in the refrigerator until ready to use or process in sterilized jars to heat seal.

RHUBARB STRAWBERRY SAUCE

Makes: 2 cups

This sauce can be served over ice cream, crepes or chocolate desserts.

8 oz. rhubarb
water to cover
8 oz. strawberries
½ cup sugar, or to taste
2 tbs. lemon juice
1 tsp. grated lemon zest

Slice rhubarb and place in the slow cooker with enough water to cover. Set cooker on low heat and cook for 1 hour or until rhubarb is tender. Strain liquid from rhubarb and puree cooked rhubarb until smooth. Add strawberries, sugar, lemon juice and peel. Puree until well mixed and smooth. Taste and adjust sweetness or tartness to personal preference.

PRUNE SAUCE

Makes 1 quart

For a delightful change, try this unique sauce on roast pork or poultry dishes.

14 oz. pitted prunes
1/4 cup lemon juice
2 tbs. grated lemon zest
18 whole cloves
1/4 tsp. cinnamon
1/4 tsp. ground allspice
1 tsp. nutmeg
about 2 cups water
1 cup sugar
1 cup vinegar, prefer balsamic

Place prunes, lemon juice, lemon peel, cloves, cinnamon, allspice and nutmeg in the slow cooker and add enough water to just cover. Cook on low heat for 45 minutes to 1 hour, until prunes are soft. When liquid has been reduced to about half the original amount, remove cloves and puree mixture with a food processor or blender. Return to slow cooker; add sugar and vinegar and cook on low heat until sugar dissolves and mixture is smooth. Taste and adjust seasoning.

HOT CRANBERRY SAUCE

Instead of opening a can and serving a cold cranberry sauce to accompany poultry or pork dishes, you may consider a hot sauce that can be spiked with a little wine or liquor.

2 cups fresh cranberries
3½ cups cranberry juice cocktail
3 tbs. cornstarch
½ cup brown sugar, packed
¼ cup lemon juice
½ cup fruity red wine, whiskey or bourbon, optional

Place cranberries and half of cranberry juice cocktail in the slow cooker on high heat. Cook until berries begin to burst, 1 to 2 hours. Dissolve cornstarch in remaining cranberry juice cocktail. Add dissolved cornstarch, brown sugar and lemon juice to mixture in cooker and turn to low. Cook until mixture begins to thicken. Turn cooker off. Add wine, taste and adjust seasonings. Serve warm.

FRUIT COMPOTE

Use this wonderful compote to serve with meat, game, poultry and even fish.

1 cup dried prunes
water to cover
1 cup drained canned peaches
1 cup drained canned pears
1 cup drained canned apricots
3 cups applesauce
2 tbs. lemon juice
1 tbs. grated lemon zest
2 tsp. cinnamon
1 tsp. ground ginger
1 tsp. nutmeg

Place dried prunes in the slow cooker with water and set cooker on high heat. Cook for 1 hour or until prunes are soft. Drain off water and add remaining ingredients. Set cooker on low heat and cook for 2 to 3 hours. Taste and adjust seasonings.

CHILI SAUCE

This is a quick, easy sauce that can be served over kebabs, fish dishes, pasta, potatoes, or even as garnish to soups and stews.

½ cup olive oil
6 large onions, chopped
12 cloves garlic
¾ cup chopped red chile peppers
1 ½ cups ketchup
salt to taste, optional

In a skillet, heat oil and sauté onions until soft. Mince garlic; seed and chop peppers and add both to onion mixture. Transfer to a food processor workbowl or blender container and puree with ketchup. Place all ingredients in the slow cooker and cook on low heat for 45 minutes to 1 hour. Taste and adjust seasonings.

PEANUT SAUCE (SATÉ SAUCE)

Makes: 4 cups

(Say SAH-TAY.) This sauce is popular to serve with Thai marinated chicken or beef skewers. It's also good over lightly sautéed chicken and fresh spinach.

¼ cup vegetable oil
2 cloves garlic, minced
1 medium onion, chopped
½ tsp. chili powder
3 lime leaves
½ tsp. curry powder
1 tbs. chopped lemon grass
1 cup coconut milk
½ cup milk
¼ tsp. cinnamon
3 bay leaves
2 tsp. tamarind paste,
   or 1 tbs. lemon juice
2 tbs. fish sauce
3 tbs. dark brown sugar
3 tbs. lemon juice
1 cup chunky peanut butter

Set the slow cooker on high heat. Heat oil and add garlic, onion, chili powder, lime leaves, curry powder and lemon grass. Cook until onion is tender. Set cooker on low heat and stir in remaining ingredients. Cook for 2 to 3 hours or until thick.

Note: Fish sauce is available in Asian markets, called *nam pla* (Thai), *nuoc nam* (Vietnamese), *patis* (Phillippines) and *shottsuru* (Japanese).

DESSERTS

HOT CHOCOLATE PUDDING

Servings: 8

This is a fudgy, rich chocolate pudding that can be mixed right in the slow cooker. If desired, serve with a dollop of whipped cream or a scoop of vanilla ice cream or frozen yogurt.

1 1/2 cups flour
1 cup sugar
3 tbs. unsweetened cocoa powder
1 tbs. baking powder
3/4 tsp. salt
3/4 cup milk
3 tbs. butter, melted
1 tsp. vanilla extract

3/4 cup brown sugar, packed
1/3 cup granulated sugar
1/4 cup unsweetened cocoa powder
1/4 tsp. salt
1 1/2 tsp. vanilla extract
1 1/2 cups boiling water
3/4 cup toasted chopped walnuts,
  optional

Mix flour, sugar, cocoa, baking powder and salt together in the slow cooker. Add milk, butter and vanilla and stir until blended. In a separate bowl, mix sugars, cocoa, salt and vanilla together and sprinkle on top of mixture in slow cooker without stirring. Pour boiling water on top. Do not mix. Set slow cooker on low heat and cook for 3 hours. If desired, just before serving, add toasted walnuts for texture.

BREAD PUDDING

This easy-to-make bread pudding will remind you of the kind of homey food Grandmother used to make on cold, wintry days.

4 cups toasted bread cubes
2½ cups scalded milk
2 eggs
¾ cup sugar
¼ tsp. cinnamon
pinch nutmeg

pinch salt
1 tsp. vanilla extract
2 tbs. butter, melted
½ cup raisins, optional
whipped cream for garnish

Put bread cubes in the slow cooker. In a bowl, mix scalded milk, eggs, sugar, cinnamon, nutmeg, salt, vanilla and melted butter. Pour mixture over bread cubes and add raisins, if desired. With the back of a spoon, gently press all bread cubes into milk mixture to make sure liquid is absorbed. Avoid stirring mixture so bread does not disintegrate. Set cooker on low heat and cook for 5 to 6 hours. Serve warm with a dollop of whipped cream, if desired.

RASPBERRY BREAD PUDDING

This is a delightful change from the standard bread pudding. Don't limit yourself to raspberries—consider using blackberries, Marionberries, loganberries, etc., for a fruity, warm winter treat.

5 cups toasted bread cubes
2½ cups milk, scalded
2 eggs
2 egg yolks
1 cup sugar

1 tsp. almond extract
2 tbs. butter, melted
12 oz. fresh or frozen raspberries
whipped cream for garnish

Place toasted bread cubes in the slow cooker. In a separate bowl, mix scalded milk, eggs, egg yolks, sugar, almond extract and melted butter together. Defrost berries; drain off any excess juice and mix berries with bread cubes. Pour milk mixture on top and gently press bread into milk mixture with the back of a spoon. Do not stir mixture. Set slow cooker on low heat and cook for 4 to 6 hours. Serve warm with a dollop of whipped cream or drizzle with *Raspberry Sauce*.

RASPBERRY SAUCE

1 pkg. (10 oz.) frozen raspberries
1/2 cup raspberry jam
few drops lemon juice
sugar, optional
1 tbs. raspberry liqueur, optional

Defrost raspberries. Place raspberries, raspberry jam and lemon juice into a food processor or blender. Puree until smooth; taste and add sugar, if desired. Strain through a sieve to remove seeds. Add raspberry liqueur, if desired. Drizzle sauce over warm *Raspberry Bread Pudding*, page 114.

PINEAPPLE BREAD PUDDING

Bring this to a party and the guests will rave.

1 cup butter, softened
2 cups sugar
1 tsp. cinnamon
8 eggs
2 cans (13½ oz. each) crushed pineapple
5 cups toasted bread cubes
½ cup chopped toasted pecans
whipped cream for garnish

In a bowl, beat butter, sugar and cinnamon until well mixed. Add eggs and beat on high until mixture is light and fluffy. Drain pineapple well and reserve juice for another use. Fold pineapple and bread cubes into creamed mixture. Pour batter into the slow cooker; set cooker on low heat for 6 to 7 hours. Before serving, sprinkle pecans on top of pudding and serve warm with a dollop of whipped cream. Serve warm.

CARAMEL BREAD PUDDING

This creamy bread pudding is smothered with caramel and toasted nuts. Try it with a dollop of whipped cream or vanilla ice cream on top.

5 cups 1-inch bread cubes, prefer
   egg bread or white bread
5 cups milk
1 cup dark or light raisins
4 eggs, beaten
1 1/2 cups sugar
1/2 tsp. cinnamon

1/8 tsp. nutmeg
1 1/2 tsp. pure vanilla extract
1/4 cup butter, melted
1/2 jar (17 oz. jar) caramel topping
1 cup chopped toasted pecans or
   walnuts, optional

Place bread cubes on a cookie sheet and toast in a 375° oven for about 15 minutes, until golden brown.

Scald milk: Heat in a saucepan on medium-high heat to just before boiling. Remove from heat. Place bread, milk, raisins, eggs, sugar, cinnamon, nutmeg, vanilla and butter in the slow cooker and cook on high heat for 1 1/2 to 1 3/4 hours, until custard is set. Pour caramel topping over cooked pudding, sprinkle with toasted nuts and serve warm.

APPLE BREAD PUDDING

Apples give bread pudding a delightful moistness and delicious flavor. Toast the bread before cooking to give it a nutty flavor. Serve with whipped cream, ice cream, frozen yogurt or other favorite topping.

8-9 pieces white or egg bread
4 tbs. butter
3 apples, prefer Golden Delicious
2 tbs. lemon juice
1 tbs. grated lemon zest

1/2-1 cup brown sugar, packed
1 tsp. cinnamon
1/4 tsp. nutmeg 1 cup apple juice
1/2 cup light raisins
1/2 cup toasted walnuts, optional

Spread bread with butter and toast both sides under a broiler. Cut bread into chunks. Place all ingredients in the slow cooker, except walnuts. The amount of sugar should be determined by tartness of apples. Set slow cooker on low heat and cook for 5 to 6 hours. If possible, stir gently halfway through cooking process. If desired, stir in toasted walnuts just before serving.

APPLE INDIAN PUDDING

Indian pudding is an old-fashioned cornmeal pudding that is strongly flavored with molasses. Apples add texture and moistness and give this dessert real substance. This is a great finale to a traditional meat-and-potatoes meal. Serve it with a dollop of whipped cream, ice cream or frozen yogurt.

2 cups milk
1/3 cup cornmeal
2 cups sliced apples, prefer Golden
    Delicious
3/4 cup molasses
1/4 cup butter, melted
1 tsp. salt

1 tsp. ground ginger
1/2 tsp. cinnamon
3 tbs. sugar
1 egg, beaten
1/2 cup light or dark raisins
whipped cream for garnish

Bring milk to a boil in a saucepan and add cornmeal. Place mixture in the slow cooker and add remaining ingredients. Amount of sugar varies depending on the type of apples used. Set slow cooker on low heat and cook for 4 to 5 hours. Allow pudding to cool to room temperature before serving—it will thicken as it cools.

CHOCOLATE WALNUT BROWNIES

When you don't have access to an oven, want to save energy, or want to keep the kitchen cool, you can bake with your slow cooker. These are great, moist brownies, and not extremely sweet.

1/2 cup butter
1 cup sugar
4 eggs
1 tsp. vanilla extract
1 can (16 oz.) chocolate syrup

1 cup flour
1/2 tsp. baking powder
1 cup chopped walnuts
2 cups water

Cream butter and sugar together. Add eggs, vanilla, chocolate syrup, flour and baking powder; beat well. Stir in walnuts. Use a coffee tin for a standard round cooker, or a loaf pan for a rectangular-shaped cooker. Grease baking pan well and pour in chocolate mixture. Set a trivet in the bottom of the slow cooker; place baking pan on top of trivet and cover pan with several layers of paper towels. Pour water into cooker. Set slow cooker on high heat and cook for about 3 to 4 hours.

Depending on depth of pan used for baking and type of cooker, time may vary; so check every 15 minutes after 3 hours for doneness. When cool, cut brownies into long slices; frost. If desired, sprinkle with additional walnuts.

CHOCOLATE FROSTING

1 cup confectioners' sugar
1/4 cup butter
1/3 cup milk
1/2 cup chocolate chips

Heat confectioners' sugar, butter and milk in a saucepan and stir until sugar is dissolved. Remove from heat; stir in chocolate chips and beat until smooth. Spread on cooled brownies.

HOLIDAY PLUM PUDDING

Servings: 12

This is a traditional English plum pudding, dark with spices and rich with fruits. If candied citron is not a favorite ingredient, substitute candied cherries or even chopped maraschino cherries. Serve with one of the hard sauces on pages 126 and 127.

8 oz. pitted dates
8 oz. dried figs
8 oz. dried apricots
8 oz. walnuts
15 oz. raisins
4 oz. chopped candied citron or
   candied cherries
1 cup sifted flour

1 tbs. pumpkin pie spice
1 tsp. salt
4 eggs
1 cup brown sugar, packed
$1/2$ lb. ground suet
$2^1/2$ cups soft white breadcrumbs
$1/2$ cup brandy
$1/2$ cup corn syrup

Butter a 10-cup mold or large coffee tin and dust with granulated sugar, tapping out any excess. Chop dates, figs, apricots and walnuts into small pieces and combine with raisins and candied citron in a large bowl. Mix flour, pumpkin pie spice and salt together and set aside. With an electric mixer, beat eggs and brown sugar together at high speed for 3 minutes until fluffy. Lower speed and mix in suet, breadcrumbs, brandy and corn syrup. Stir in flour mixture until well blended. Pour mixture over fruit and nut mixture; stir until well blended.

Spoon into prepared mold, cover with foil and fasten with string. Place mold in the slow cooker and fill cooker with water to halfway up mold. Set cooker on high heat and cook for 6 to 7 hours. When done, a skewer inserted into the center of pudding should come out clean. Cool pudding in mold for 30 minutes before removing. Serve warm or at room temperature with hard sauce.

HARD SAUCES

This trio of hard sauces offers variations for holiday puddings and other cake-type desserts. In England, hard sauce is known as "brandy butter."

TRADITIONAL HARD SAUCE
$1/2$ cup butter, room temperature
2 cups confectioners' sugar
$1/4$ tsp. salt
2 tbs. brandy, rum or whiskey, or more to taste

With an electric beater or food processor, beat butter until smooth. Sift confectioners' sugar and add to butter, beating well. Add salt and chosen liquor. Add additional liquor, if desired. Chill until ready to use; bring to room temperature before serving.

FRUITED HARD SAUCE

2/3 cups butter, room temperature
2 1/3 cups confectioners' sugar
1/2 cup cream

1 1/3 cups crushed berries, chopped maraschino cherries or mashed bananas
1 tbs. berry-flavored liqueur, amaretto or banana liqueur, optional

With an electric mixer or food processor, beat butter until smooth. Sift confectioners' sugar and add to butter, beating well. Beat in cream and add crushed fruit, beating well. If desired, beat in a liqueur that complements fruit used. Chill.

SPICY HARD SAUCE

1/2 cup butter, room temperature
2 cups confectioners' sugar
1/4 tsp. salt
1 tsp. cinnamon

1/2 tsp. ground cloves
pinch nutmeg
1/2 cup cream
1-2 tbs. liquor or liqueur of choice

With an electric mixer or food processor, beat butter until soft. Sift confectioners' sugar and add to butter, beating well. Add remaining ingredients, beating well. Chill.

CRANBERRY PUDDING

This is similar to steamed plum pudding, but more colorful and fresher-tasting. If you freeze fresh cranberries when they are plentiful, or find frozen cranberries in the freezer case, you can have this dessert year-round. Top with Butter Sauce, page 129, or one of the hard sauces on pages 126 and 127.

2 cups fresh or frozen, defrosted
   cranberries
1 1/2 cups flour
1/2 cup molasses, prefer light

1/2 cup boiling water
2 tsp. baking soda
1/4 tsp. salt
1 tsp. grated orange zest

Coarsely chop cranberries and mix with flour (this helps prevent the berries from sinking to the bottom of the pudding during steaming). Mix molasses, water, soda, salt and orange zest together; stir into cranberries.

Grease a pudding mold or large coffee tin, pour in pudding mixture, cover with waxed paper and tie tightly with string. Place in the slow cooker and pour water into cooker halfway up outside of mold. Set cooker on high heat and cook for 5 to 6 hours. When done, a knife inserted in the center should come out clean. Serve warm or at room temperature.

BUTTER SAUCE

Makes 1 quart

This is delicious over Cranberry Pudding, *page 128.*

1 cup sugar
1/2 cup butter

1/2 cup cream
1 tsp. vanilla extract or grated orange
    zest

In a heavy-bottomed saucepan or double boiler, slowly heat sugar, butter and cream until sugar is dissolved. With an electric mixer, whip at high speed until thickened. Stir in vanilla or orange zest.

SIMPLE FUDGE SAUCE

Makes 1 quart

Use this as a sauce or as a dessert fondue for dipping fruits and cake chunks.

12 oz. semi-sweet chocolate chips
1/4 cup butter
2 cans (14 oz. each) sweetened
    condensed milk

1/3 cup liqueur: amaretto, orange-
    flavored, Frangelico, coffee or mint,
    optional

Place chocolate chips, butter and condensed milk in the slow cooker. Set cooker on low heat and cook for 1 to 2 hours; stir occasionally until chocolate melts. Stir in liqueur, if desired. Serve directly from slow cooker or serve warm over desserts.

CHOCOLATE ALMOND TRUFFLES

Allow the fudge sauce to cool to room temperature and it will solidify to the consistency of a truffle. Use mint, Frangelico or orange liqueurs for flavorings.

1 recipe *Simple Fudge Sauce*, page 129
amaretto liqueur or almond flavoring to taste
1 cup finely chopped toasted almonds

Bring fudge sauce to room temperature to solidify. Add amaretto and stir. With a small ice cream scoop or lemon baller, scoop out chocolate into balls about walnut size. Drop onto a plate with finely chopped toasted almonds and roll, coating each ball thoroughly. Refrigerate until ready to serve.

CREAMY ORANGE FONDUE

Don't be limited in thinking dessert fondues can only be chocolate. This is a creamy, simple dessert that can be served with fresh fruit, canned fruit or cake.

1/4 cup butter
1/4 cup flour
1 1/2 cups half-and-half
1/4 cup sugar
1 tbs. grated orange zest
8 oz. cream cheese
1/2 cup orange-flavored liqueur, optional

In the slow cooker on high heat, melt butter and whisk in flour to form a paste. Slowly stir in half-and-half until smooth. Add sugar and orange zest and stir. Set slow cooker on low heat. Cube cream cheese and stir into cream mixture. Cook, stirring occasionally, until cream cheese melts, about 1 hour. Stir in liqueur, if desired.

CHOCOLATE ESPRESSO SAUCE

This is a rich, not overly sweet sauce that is great for dipping cakes or fruit or as a topping for ice cream. This sauce can also be cooled and used with ice cream pie or frozen desserts.

12 oz. unsweetened chocolate, finely chopped
2²/₃ cups hot espresso coffee
3 cups sugar
¹/₂ cup amaretto liqueur
¹/₂ cup butter

Place chocolate in the slow cooker. Mix espresso coffee and sugar together, pour over chocolate and stir. Set slow cooker on low heat and cook until chocolate is melted and smooth, stirring occasionally, about 45 minutes to 1 hour. Add amaretto and butter; stir until smooth and glossy. Serve over ice cream or keep warm and use as a dessert fondue.

APPLE DATE PUDDING

This delicious, easy-to-fix, warm dessert can be topped with whipped cream or ice cream.

4-5 apples, peeled, cored and diced
3/4 cup sugar, or less, to taste
1/2 cup chopped dates
1/2 cup chopped toasted pecans
2 tbs. flour
1 tsp. baking powder
1/8 tsp. salt
1/4 tsp. nutmeg
2 tbs. butter, melted
1 egg, beaten

In the slow cooker, place apples, sugar, dates and pecans; stir. In a separate bowl, mix together flour, baking powder, salt and nutmeg and stir into apple mixture. Drizzle melted butter over batter and stir. Stir in egg. Set cooker on low heat and cook for 3 to 4 hours. Serve warm.

Note: If crisper nuts are desired, add toasted pecans at the end of cooking period.

FILLED PEARS IN WINE

This is a popular, light dessert made even more special with a delicious filling.

6 firm Danjou or Bosc pears
2 cups dry red wine
1 cup sugar
1 tsp. grated lemon zest
1 1/2 tsp. cornstarch
1 tbs. water

1/2 cup chopped almonds
1 tbs. sugar
1/2 cup crushed macaroons, vanilla
   wafers or toasted ladyfingers
whipped cream for garnish

Peel pears, cut a thin slice from the bottoms so they stand up by themselves and place them in the slow cooker. Mix together wine, sugar and lemon zest and pour over pears. Set slow cooker on low heat and cook for 4 to 6 hours. To test for doneness, pears should be easy to pierce with a sharp knife, but not mushy. Remove pears and allow to cool. Set cooker on high heat. Mix cornstarch with water. When wine mixture begins to bubble, add cornstarch mixture and stir until thickened. Mix almonds, sugar and crushed macaroons together. When pears are cool enough to handle, core them with an apple corer, leaving pears whole. Drizzle with glaze. You may have to glaze several times to achieve a thick coating on pears. Carefully fill pears with almond-macaroon mixture. Serve with a dollop of whipped cream.

APRICOTS IN ALMOND LIQUEUR

Servings: 6

This quick and simple dessert is delightful after a heavy meal.

1 can (19 oz.) whole apricots
1 tbs. cornstarch
$1/2$ cup amaretto liqueur
whipped cream for garnish
toasted slivered almonds for garnish

Drain apricots and place juice in the slow cooker with cornstarch. Stir to dissolve. Set cooker on low heat and allow mixture to thicken, half an hour to 1 hour. Add amaretto and cook another 30 minutes. Pour sauce over apricots; cover and refrigerate for several hours. Garnish with whipped cream and a sprinkling of toasted almonds.

MARBLED CHOCOLATE CREAM CHEESE CAKE

Servings: 6

This dark, moist cake is swirled with creamy cheese. To vary, add 1/3 cup toasted coconut to the cream cheese mixture.

4 oz. cream cheese
1/2 beaten egg
1/4 cup sugar
pinch salt
1/2 cup milk chocolate or semi-sweet
  chocolate chips
1 1/2 cups flour
1 tsp. soda

1/2 tsp. salt
1 cup sugar
1/4 cup cocoa powder
1 cup water
1/2 cup vegetable oil
1 tbs. vinegar
1 1/2 tsp. pure vanilla extract

In a bowl, beat cream cheese, egg, sugar and salt together until smooth. Stir in chocolate chips. In a separate bowl, combine flour, soda, salt, sugar and cocoa powder. Beat in water, oil, vinegar and vanilla until just blended.

For easy removal, line slow cooker with aluminum foil and pour chocolate mixture into foil liner. Place tablespoonfuls of cream cheese mixture in dollops on the chocolate mixture and with a table knife, gently swirl mixtures together to create a marbled design. Set cooker on high heat and cook for about 2 hours or until a knife inserted in the center comes out clean.

SUPER MOIST BROWNIES

This rich, gooey brownie is always a great hit at parties. If you choose to add nuts, try a change by using toasted macadamia nuts or pecans.

1 ½ cups sugar
1 cup dark brown sugar, packed
1 cup butter
4 squares (1 oz. each) unsweetened
  chocolate, grated
2 tbs. light corn syrup

1 cup flour
1 ¼ tsp. baking powder
4 eggs
2 tsp. pure vanilla extract
2-4 cups chopped toasted walnuts,
  optional

Place sugars, butter, grated chocolate and corn syrup in a saucepan and cook on medium high, stirring constantly until smooth. Remove from heat and cool to room temperature. The gently stir in flour, baking powder, eggs, vanilla and nuts (if desired). For easy removal, line bottom third of slow cooker with aluminum foil and pour brownie mixture into the foil. Set slow cooker on high heat and cook for about 2 hours or until a knife inserted in the center comes out clean. Immediately remove from cooker and cool to room temperature before cutting.

MAPLE APPLE CRISP

Toasting the oats gives the topping a nutty flavor and helps to maintain some crispness. Serve with a scoop of vanilla ice cream and a drizzle of maple syrup.

5 large apples: Golden Delicious, Newton, Pippin or Granny Smith
$1/2$ cup maple syrup
$1/2$ tsp. cinnamon
$1/2$ tsp. nutmeg
1 tbs. lemon juice
$1/2$ cup chopped dried apricots or raisins, optional
$1 1/2$ cups rolled oats
$1/2$ cup flour
$1/2$ cup brown sugar, packed
$1/2$ cup sugar
pinch salt
1 tsp. pure vanilla extract
$1/2$ cup butter

Pare, core and slice apples about $1/8$ inch thick. Place apples, maple syrup, cinnamon, nutmeg, lemon juice and dried apricots in the slow cooker and stir to mix. Set cooker on high heat.

Prepare topping: Spread oats onto a baking sheet and place under the broiler until oats turn a light brown; watch very carefully. Remove from oven and cool slightly.

In a bowl, place flour, brown sugar, sugar, salt, and vanilla. With a pastry blender, cut in butter (as you would when making pie dough), until butter pieces are about the size of peas. Stir in cooled oats and pour mixture into center of apples, spreading mixture to within $1/2$-inch of edge of cooker. This will allow the moisture from the apples to escape and keep the topping from getting too soggy. Bake on high heat until apples are tender, about $1 3/4$ hours. Best served warm.

EASY PUMPKIN CHEESECAKE

Servings: 8

The baking mix added to the recipe will give the appearance of a small crust.

1 pkg. (8 oz.) cream cheese, softened
3/4 cup sugar
1/2 cup Bisquick (or baking mix)
1 1/2 tsp. ground cinnamon
1/2 tsp. nutmeg
1/2 tsp. ground ginger

1/2 tsp. pure vanilla extract
1 tbs. grated orange zest, or 1 tsp.
  dried orange peel
3 eggs
1 can (16 oz.) pumpkin

TOPPING

1 cup sour cream
3 tbs. sugar

2 tsp. pure vanilla extract

With a food processor or mixer, beat cream cheese until smooth. Add sugar, baking mix, spices, vanilla, orange peel, eggs and pumpkin and beat until smooth and creamy. Line the slow cooker with aluminum foil over bottom and about 3 inches up sides. Pour mixture inside foil and cook on high heat for about 1 1/2 to 1 3/4 hours or until center of cheesecake just begins to look solid. In a bowl, mix together sour cream, sugar and vanilla. Gently remove cheesecake from cooker and pour sour cream mixture on top. Cool to room temperature. When cheesecake is cool, refrigerate for at least 3 to 4 hours before serving.

RICE PUDDING

To add dimension to this pudding, soak the raisins in dark rum or your favorite liqueur. In place of raisins, you can use chopped dates, lychee nuts with a few maraschino cherries or even fresh berries. Carefully stir additions in after the mixture has cooked and cooled.

3 cups milk
1 1/2 tbs. butter, melted
1/2-3/4 cup sugar
1/3 tsp. salt

3 eggs, beaten
3/4 tsp. pure vanilla extract
1 1/2 cups cooked rice
1 cup raisins, optional

Place milk, melted butter, sugar, salt, eggs and vanilla directly into the slow cooker and beat with a whisk until well mixed. Gently stir in rice and raisins, if desired.

Set slow cooker on high heat and cook for 1 3/4 to 2 hours or until mixture looks creamy and slightly thick; pudding will thicken as it cools. Turn off cooker and cool mixture to room temperature, and then refrigerate until ready to eat.

Note: You will be tempted to add more rice to the recipe because it looks "soupy," but be aware that the rice will absorb the milk and the mixture will thicken as it cooks.

EGG CUSTARD

This is a favorite dessert that my mother used to fix. Serve it with a small dollop of sweetened whipped cream and with fresh or canned fruit, if desired.

4 whole eggs
2/3 cup sugar
1/2 tsp. salt
4 cups milk, scalded
1 tsp. vanilla extract
1/4-1/2 tsp. nutmeg

With a mixer or food processor, beat eggs, sugar and salt together until well blended. Add scalded milk (which has been heated until just before boiling and removed from heat), vanilla and nutmeg. When mixture is completely blended, pour into the slow cooker and cook on high heat for 1¾ to 2 hours or until a knife inserted in the center comes out clean. Chill until ready to serve.

FRUITED PUDDING

Serve this old-fashioned dessert with a dollop of whipped cream or vanilla ice cream. You can vary this recipe by adding a chopped banana along with the fruit cocktail and substituting banana extract for the vanilla.

1¼ cups flour
1 cup sugar
1 tsp. baking soda
¼ tsp. salt
1 egg, beaten

1 can (15 oz.) fruit cocktail, undrained
1 tsp. pure vanilla extract
½ cup dark brown sugar, packed
½ cup chopped, toasted pecans or
   walnuts

Combine flour, sugar, baking soda and salt in a bowl and set aside. In a separate bowl, mix together egg, fruit cocktail (including syrup) and vanilla. Gently stir egg mixture with dry ingredients until just barely mixed and pour into the slow cooker. In a small bowl, stir together brown sugar and nuts and sprinkle over batter. Set cooker on high heat and cook for about 2 hours or until knife inserted in the center comes out clean. Best served warm.

COCONUT CHEESE FUDGE CAKE

Servings: 10-12

This quick, moist chocolate cake has a coconut cream cheese filling. It's rich enough to serve without a frosting, but I have included a recipe for a chocolate cream cheese frosting if you really are going for decadence!

1 pkg. (18 oz.) chocolate fudge cake mix
1 1/4 cups water
1/2 cup sour cream
2 eggs
1/2 tsp. vanilla extract
8 oz. cream cheese, softened
2 eggs
3 cup sugar
1 cup coconut

Cut a round of brown paper or parchment to fit into the bottom of the slow cooker. With a mixer, beat cake mix, water, sour cream, eggs and vanilla together for 2 minutes. In a separate bowl, beat together cream cheese, eggs and sugar until smooth. Add coconut and beat just until mixed. Pour 2/3 of the chocolate mixture into the slow cooker, spread with cream cheese mixture and top with remaining chocolate mixture.

Bake on high heat for 2 hours. To remove, cut around the edge with a sharp knife, turn cooker on its side and gently allow cake to fall out. When cake is cool, spread with chocolate cream cheese frosting.

CHOCOLATE CREAM CHEESE FROSTING
3 oz. pkg. cream cheese, softened
1 tbs. milk
2½ cups sifted confectioners' sugar
2 oz. unsweetened chocolate, melted
1 tsp. vanilla extract
dash salt

With a mixer or food processor, beat cream cheese and milk together until smooth. Add confectioners' sugar, chocolate, vanilla and salt. Beat until smooth and spread on completely cooled cake.

CHERRY TEACAKE WITH CHERRY BUTTER

Servings: 8

If fresh cherries are not available, use dried cherries that have been rehydrated for several minutes in boiling water or in a cherry-flavored liqueur.

2¹/₂ cups flour, sifted
2 tsp. baking powder
1 tsp. cinnamon
¹/₂ tsp. baking soda
¹/₂ tsp. salt
¹/₂ tsp. ground allspice
¹/₄ cup butter
1 cup brown sugar, packed
1 egg, beaten
1 cup chopped dark sweet cherries
³/₄ cup sour cream
¹/₄ cup orange juice
1 tbs. grated orange zest, or 1 tsp. dried orange peel
³/₄ cup chopped toasted walnuts or pecans
Cherry Butter, follows

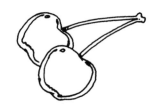

In a bowl, mix together flour, baking powder, cinnamon, baking soda, salt and allspice and set aside. With a mixer, beat butter and brown sugar together until smooth. Add egg and beat mixture until light and fluffy. Gently stir in cherries, sour cream, orange juice, orange peel and nuts. Add flour mixture and stir until just barely mixed. Cut a round of brown paper or parchment to fit the bottom of the slow cooker and pour mixture on top. Set slow cooker on high heat and cook for about 2 hours or until a knife inserted in the center comes out clean. To remove, run a knife around edge of cake, turn cooker on its side and gently allow cake to fall out. Best served warm with *Cherry Butter*.

CHERRY BUTTER

To enhance the cherry flavor, add a few drops of cherry flavoring or amaretto liqueur.

$^1/_2$ cup butter
$^1/_2$ cup brown sugar, packed
1 tbs. fresh lemon juice
$^1/_2$ cup chopped dark cherries

With a food processor or mixer, beat butter, brown sugar and lemon juice together until smooth. Add cherries and just barely blend. Serve at room temperature.

POTPOURRI

Fill your slow cooker half full of water, add flowers and spices and other aromatics, set the cooker on low heat (leaving the lid off) — and fill your house with delightful aromas. You can add one or two cups of commercially prepared potpourri, or make your own potpourri with one of the two recipes included here. The potpourri that include spices are the most effective in the slow cooker.

SPICY POTPOURRI

Fill your house full of a spicy aroma of cloves, cinnamon and nutmeg — ideal for the holidays.

8 cups dried rose petals
2 cups dried lavender flowers
2 tsp. anise seed
2 tbs. whole cloves
2 tbs. nutmeg
2 tbs. coarsely crushed cinnamon stick

2 tbs. crushed fixative, prefer benzoin*
10 drops jasmine oil
10 drops rose geranium oil
10 drops patchouli oil
10 drops rosemary oil

Mix all ingredients together well and place in a dark container or preferably store in glass in a dark cupboard. Allow to season for 1 month before using.

Fill the slow cooker half full of water. Toss in 1 or 2 cups of seasoned potpourri. Set on low heat and leave lid off cooker. The aroma will fill your house and help create a holiday memory.

*The flower oils used are essential volatile oils that can be obtained from craft stores, health food stores, etc. Fixatives are used to maintain the fragrance of the ingredients. They absorb the oils and retard evaporation. Fixatives like benzoin or tonka bean are available at craft stores or floral shops.

LAVENDER POTPOURRI

Makes 2¼ pound

This potpourri is delicate and reminiscent of "the olden days." Besides using it in the slow cooker as a room freshener, this mix can be used to fill sachets.

1 lb. dried lavender flowers
2 oz. dried sweet woodruff
1½ oz. dried thyme
1½ oz. dried moss, any fragrant variety
8 oz. slivered orange zest
½ cup crushed benzoin fixative *
2 oz. dried violet flowers
1 tbs. whole cloves
1 tbs. anise seed

Mix all ingredients together well. Place in a dark container or preferably store in glass in a dark place. Allow to season for 1 month.

Fill the slow cooker half full of water and toss in 1 to 2 cups of potpourri mix. Set on low heat without the lid, allowing the house to fill with this delightful aroma.

* Floral fixatives (like benzoin) can be found at craft or floral stores.

INDEX

Serve Creative, Easy, Nutritious Meals with nitty gritty® Cookbooks

100 Dynamite Desserts
The 9 x 13 Pan Cookbook
The Barbecue Cookbook *(new)*
Beer and Good Food
The Best Bagels are Made at Home
The Best Pizza is Made at Home *(new)*
Bread Baking
Bread Machine Cookbook
Bread Machine Cookbook II
Bread Machine Cookbook III
Bread Machine Cookbook IV
Bread Machine Cookbook V
Bread Machine Cookbook VI
Cappuccino/Espresso
Casseroles *(new)*
The Coffee Book
Convection Oven Cookery *(new)*
Cooking for 1 or 2
Cooking in Clay
Cooking in Porcelain
Cooking with Chile Peppers
Cooking with Grains
Cooking with Your Kids
Creative Mexican Cooking
Deep Fried Indulgences

The Dehydrator Cookbook
Easy Vegetarian Cooking
Edible Pockets for Every Meal
Entrées From Your Bread Machine
Extra-Special Crockery Pot Recipes
Fabulous Fiber Cookery
Fondue and Hot Dips
Fresh Vegetables
From Freezer, 'Fridge and Pantry
From Your Ice Cream Maker
The Garlic Cookbook
Gourmet Gifts
Healthy Cooking on the Run
Healthy Snacks for Kids
Indoor Grilling
The Juicer Book
The Juicer Book II
Lowfat American Favorites
Marinades
Muffins, Nut Breads and More
The New Blender Book
New International Fondue Cookbook
No Salt, No Sugar, No Fat
One-Dish Meals
Oven and Rotisserie Roasting

Party Fare
The Pasta Machine Cookbook
Pinch of Time: Meals in Less than 30
    Minutes
Quick and Easy Pasta Recipes
Recipes for the Loaf Pan
Recipes for the Pressure Cooker
Recipes for Yogurt Cheese
Risottos, Paellas, and other Rice
    Specialties
The Sandwich Maker Cookbook
The Sensational Skillet: Sautés and
    Stir-Fries *(new)*
Slow Cooking in Crock-Pot,® Slow
    Cooker, Oven and Multi-Cooker
The Steamer Cookbook
The Toaster Oven Cookbook
Unbeatable Chicken Recipes
The Versatile Rice Cooker
Waffles
The Well Dressed Potato
The Wok
Worldwide Sourdoughs from Your
    Bread Machine
Wraps and Roll-Ups

For a free catalog, call: Bristol Publishing Enterprises, Inc.
(800) 346-4889
www.bristolcookbooks.com